...ungs
Over Milestones

Meanings Over Milestones

Mothers
Sharing
Beliefs, Values, Purpose
and Passion
with Their Children

The Positive
Motherhood Project™

Edited by
Angharad Davies

TP
MP

First published in 2021 by The Positive Motherhood Project Ltd
www.thepositivemotherhoodproject.com

ISBN: 978-1-5262-0887-3

Cover design and typesetting: Fuzzy Flamingo
www.fuzzyflamingo.co.uk

This book is a collection of creative non-fiction. The stories in this book are based on the reality and opinions of the authors who contributed their individual experiences. They represent one side of a story. The Positive Motherhood Project Ltd can't confirm that all the events of these stories are factual and have done everything possible to protect all parties involved. Through recounting their life stories the authors have in no way intended to lay blame or cause offense to any person connected to their life events.

This book deals with issues such as loss, mental health, physical illness and infertility that the reader may find distressing. Discretion is advised.

To our mothers.
To those seeds of life meanings and beliefs that you gave us to water, weed and wish upon.
Thank you.

Contents

Preface

I invite you to imagine a world where life meaning is just as important as life milestones. A world where beliefs, values, purpose and passion are the driving force for children all over.

This is the world I want to see. And to get there I have started with mums!

I want to inspire mums everywhere to look inwards, reflect on their values, beliefs, purpose and passions and share these with their children.

This book asks the question, "What one life meaning would you love your child to learn from you?" And in it, you'll find the answers of over sixty mums, writers and amateurs alike.

This is a book that has been co-written and crowdfunded. A book that shares memoirs of strength, vulnerability and motherly wisdom. A book that all mums of children of any age can relate to and find inspiration from. A book that has over sixty different voices, but one unified purpose: to share with our children the life meanings we hold most true.

It is also a book that I hope will make a difference to a generation of children worldwide as we are dedicating every penny of profits to supporting global grass-roots projects for children's emotional well-being.

Now, take a well-earned break, put the kettle on and enjoy this collection of messages and meaning from mother to child.

Many many thanks,

Angharad

Founder of The Positive Motherhood Project™

If you'd like to share your story, please visit:
www.meaningsovermilestones.me

Love Never Dies

Shammy Walton

For my daughter,

Life can be so hard sometimes, it can be a struggle to get out of bed.

Since your dad passed away, I've had to remember how grateful I am to have had his love at all. When I miss him and I get that awful churning feeling in the pit of my stomach, I have to remember some people don't feel love like I had with him in a lifetime. I have to remind myself how blessed I have been.

I love love. It's the best feeling in the world. Feeling love brings so much joy. That feeling you get when someone you love smiles back at you. It fills your heart and makes you feel so warm inside. The feeling of being home, secure and happy to be alive.

My first true love was my mum. Her smile could light up a room, her energy was infectious. She was beautiful inside and out, a human rights activist and counsellor. She was full of empathy and compassion. When I lost her, as a child, I remember feeling lost. My heart was broken for a very long time. It still is.

When I was a kid, I used to close my eyes and picture her arms around me. I would remember how her love felt and it would make me smile. I still do this when I miss her.

More recently I lost my soulmate, your father. His big blue eyes could see deep into my soul. Sometimes he could just look at me and know exactly what I was thinking. He was my other half and together we were one. His smile made me melt.

Our connection was one that some people don't get to experience in a lifetime. So, although I miss him every day, I am so grateful to have had this love.

You were born out of absolute soul-wrenching love. I have never been in love like I was with your father. Our love was a soul connection, it was so much more than just a physical connection. Sometimes our love was so strong I felt like I left my body.

His love healed me and made me a better person. Sean's love made me want to be the best version of me that I can.

When Dad's cancer got bad, he asked my permission to leave, and I gave it. As much as I wanted to say no, he had to be free from pain, without guilt. This is love.

I want you to remember that, when you are missing Daddy, his energy surrounds you every day. He is always with us. I know it's not the same, but close your eyes and remember how his love makes you feel. Spray his aftershave and picture his love.

When I look at you my heart bursts with happiness. This is love. All my pain just melts away in that moment.

Love hurts when someone leaves but understand that love is eternal. Love is the only thing that lasts forever.

Shammy Alia Walton lives in Manchester with her five-year-old daughter. A web designer by trade, she lives for holistic therapies and is a qualified reiki practitioner. She lost her thirty-four-year old husband to cancer in October 2019 after a short battle with the disease. Her bond with her daughter has always been strong, but since going through this loss, it holds no bounds. Her daughter literally saved her life.

Commit Before You're Ready and Your Life Will Be Bold

Charlotte Tarrant

Inside the Taj Mahal, a man with a round face and orange cap asks where my husband and children are. He is Imran, my guide. From sunrise, he has enlightened me about this exquisite mausoleum, Shah Jahan's promise to Mumtaz Mahal on her deathbed. Imran has revealed the symmetry of this paradise complex, offset only by the emperor's tomb. He has pointed to shimmering marble and polished stones. And he has spoken with such pride about Mumtaz, a philanthropist who helped widows and orphans, mother to fourteen children, seven of whom died. Such generous storytelling deserves reciprocity.

'So, tell me about you, Madam. Are you married?' This time, I tell Imran about my (fictional) husband Adam (invented in a Malaysian market).

'Why is Adam not here with you? You cannot come to the Taj Mahal alone.'

'He's flying to India after a photoshoot. Any day now.'

'And how many children do you have?'

'We don't have children.'

Imran stops. He turns and wobbles his head. 'But Madam, you must have a child. You must have a child right now.'

'Here? At the Taj Mahal?'

'Really, Madam. It is most important.'

I smile. 'Okay, Imran, will do.' A flock of schoolchildren in white clothing pass by. They are little birds with agile limbs and bare feet. Seeing their lightness, my throat contracts. I hold tight until I say goodbye to Imran. The Yamuna river breeze is like welcome water.

Imran is right, of course. Becoming a mother is most important for me. But now I see the catalogue of commitment phobia too. Aged thirty-four, I am four years' single. I'm travelling solo in Asia, pursuing fun and freedom. Have I cherry-picked life's easy wins? Academic work, I have aced predictably (when focused). But what of creative writing? I have boxed up untold words. And the desk jobs of my twenties? Those windowless rooms! I couldn't stay longer than eighteen months. Money, I have made it in waves and splashed it, never saved. Relationships? I have managed two medium-termers but, as my friends are marrying and having babies, I'm selling my possessions and packing a rucksack for Bangkok.

Unexpected feeling: is this the springboard of change? This day, Imran taps an extraordinary love – painful in this moment, yes, but now airborne, undeniable. After the tour, I stay on at the Taj Mahal. I sit on cool marble ground. A gardener in a smart shirt tends star-shaped beds and snips blades on the lawn. Another man scoops cuttings into hessian bags, emptying them into a box on his cycle-rickshaw. The whirr of the mower and the smell of cut grass are restful. An Indian palm squirrel darts up a big leaf mahogany tree, where he squeaks at a mate. And the Taj Mahal transforms across the day: shell pink at sunrise; white glitter at noon; burnt orange at sundown. I anticipate the silhouette dome against the burgundy haze at nightfall. 20,000 workers, 1,000 elephants, 22 years: to create this magnificent proof of commitment's power.

Ten years on, to my three-year-old rainbow girl, I say this: be the tortoise. Above all, start. Don't search for certainty – it's a mirage! Plod; make mistakes; take breaks; then walk on. Arrive first or last. It really doesn't matter. As long as you choose, dear Natalie, you will experience life in primary colours.

Charlotte Tarrant lives with her partner Phil and daughter Natalie in Hertfordshire, UK. She's a freelance writer and the founder of Starlike Books. The company exists to cheer on, gift and create children's books that inspire courage, hope, love and joy. Charlotte posts letters on a blog to her late father, John, who still encourages her to write with heart and commitment. Charlotte's mum, Elizabeth, continues to pass on her lifelong love of reading. If you enjoy picture books, strong tea and splashes of universal wonder, please say hello to Charlotte at Starlike Books on Instagram.

Even the Darkest Clouds Can Have Silver Linings

Rose Child

The first months of my daughter's life were the worst months of mine. Even now, after several years and lots of therapy, that still hurts to write. A couple of days after she was born, things began to fall apart in my mind. I felt constantly terrified, refused to sleep, and wouldn't leave my daughter for even a moment. When she was eight days old, the situation – and I – became desperate. To save my life, my daughter and I were admitted to a psychiatric mother and baby unit a hundred miles from our home. I continued to have extreme anxiety, was unable to sleep without sedation, and had episodes of near-catatonic depression. We were discharged after two months, but I remained very unwell at home for some time. My daughter was around six months before my mental health was anything approaching stable.

In such a vulnerable state, it would be understandable for our brains to equate illness caused by having a baby with illness caused by the baby itself. There would be no fault in us for that. But I'll remain forever thankful that my brain never made that connection. For me, and for many women I've encountered who've suffered from acute perinatal mental illness, our babies are what kept us alive.

I loved my daughter intensely. My only smiles were for her. Holding her made me feel like I was doing one small bit of good in the world. But my mind felt like it was disintegrating, and I couldn't see a way through. All I wanted was what was best for her. And all I wanted was to be her mother. But those two things seemed completely at odds. Who would want a mother who cried constantly and got admitted to psychiatric units when everyone else just seemed to cope?

My daughter, as it turned out.

To recover as fully as I did, I had support, and medication, and therapy, and time. But most of all, I had my daughter. She is what gave me the determination to seek and accept the help that I so desperately needed. She is what got me out of bed every day. Quite literally. And under her constant, trusting gaze, I was gradually able to see what she so clearly saw – that I was someone worth loving. Someone doing their absolute best for her. Her mother.

Far from being what caused my illness, my daughter is what saved me from it. She is here because of me, yes. But I am also here because of her. I will always be grateful to her, and grateful for her.

While I can never be glad about what happened to me, I can still appreciate that it has made me the person I am today and forged the unbreakable bond that my daughter and I have. There is a marked difference between the toxic positivity that often gets aimed at people when they've been through something like this, and a genuine, hard-won appreciation that the most wonderful things really can come out of the worst of experiences.

To my daughter (although I hope she'll never need to hear it), and to anyone else in the darkest of places: don't give up. On the other side of this there is more love than you can hold.

Rose Child lives in Bristol, UK, with her partner and daughter. After experiencing acute postpartum mental illness, she left her long-term career to work, write and research in the field of perinatal mental health. You can find more of Rose's writing on her blog, Mother Courage.

Understand You, Embrace You, Be You

Allie Atkinson

To my three luminaries,

If I could teach you to do one thing as you grow, it would be to learn who you are and to live authentically. Because it is only now, as a grown woman in my thirties and with three young children relying on me, that I realise the importance of loving yourself unconditionally.

Becoming a mum changed my life completely but as well as feeling an overwhelming amount of love, it has left me feeling very lost. Anxiety and low self-esteem have dominated me. Every cry, every missed naptime, every nappy change struggle has left me feeling frustrated and useless as a woman. And gradually, those feelings have consumed me. The fun activities have become rarer out of fear that someone may hurt themselves or something could get broken and messy amongst the excitement. I've watched other mums create such magic with their own little ones whilst I've felt unable to compete. But with all this avoidance and comparison, comes shame and guilt, and the vicious circle continues.

It is those feelings that have led me, with the help of therapy, to begin studying who I am and why I feel that way. And I've come to realise the significance of our core beliefs, our personality types, our coping methods and our thinking patterns. The truth is, I've actually spent most of my life comparing myself to others, wanting to look like others or dress like others, or react like others to situations. Be stronger. Be softer. More talkative. Less talkative. I built perfectionist coping methods from a young age meaning I needed to achieve at school, wow at dance and thrive in work as evidence that I was doing well and that I was worthy. And when I became your mum and chose to stay at home with you, those constant outside validations disappeared and the coping methods no longer worked. As any mum will tell you, we're all winging it and sometimes we have no idea if we are doing it right, and gradually that uncertainty has chipped away at me. But I hope that as I continue to learn about myself, that need for external approval will disappear and I will listen to my own voice instead.

So, I hope that you will know who you are before you reach the stage I have. Take the time to study yourself. Find out if you have a logical mind or a creative mind or even both. Discover what makes you smile from the inside and what triggers you to feel upset, or angry. If you're a perfectionist, dig deeper and learn why. If you procrastinate, question yourself. Know yourself so well that you understand that you can never compare yourself to someone else because you are made to be individual. Be comfortable with the idea that some people will think you talk too much, and others will think you're too quiet, but the right people will love you regardless. Grow. Push yourself to face your fears and trust your instincts. And most importantly embrace it all, every fragment, so that you have the confidence and the self-belief to be yourself unapologetically and live your best life without the approval of others.

This is my wish for you.

Allie Atkinson lives in Leicestershire with her husband and is a stay-at-home mummy to their three children. In addition to other writing opportunities, Allie has her own blog, 'Just One Mama', sharing her thoughts and feelings on motherhood experiences, alongside monthly guest writers, to provide support, comfort and inspiration to others.

Anything Is Possible If Only You Believe

Maria Honeker

I always knew I wanted to become a mum. When the time came to start trying for a baby, I was bursting with excitement. Pregnancy, however, turned out to be anything but a joyful experience. Every time I got pregnant, we found ourselves on cloud nine, only to miscarry weeks later. Months of trying turned into years and eventually we needed help to achieve and sustain a pregnancy. We were determined to make parenthood happen and even made it our goal one year to become parents.

During our fertility treatment, I donated some of my eggs to a woman who was unable to have children of her own. Ironically, my pregnancy ended up in yet another miscarriage and the woman who received my eggs became pregnant with twins. Despite our loss, it was such a blessing knowing that I had brought so much joy to someone else. I had the opportunity to write the unborn babies a note and knowing that one day they would read it felt magical. The news of the woman's pregnancy was a beautiful, yet bittersweet, reminder that anything is possible, even when you feel all is lost.

A few months later our fertility journey took us to my native Sweden. This time I knew we were destined for success. Everything felt right and, despite living in England, heading home for the procedure felt like an obvious choice. This is when you were conceived, dear Isaac, on a gorgeous sunny spring day. We had longed for you for so long and when we found out we were having a boy, the name Isaac felt like the obvious choice. It means the one who laughs, and you really have brought joy to so many.

We wanted a sibling for you, but we thought it would never happen, so we stopped trying. Two and a half years later, you came along Elliot as a pleasant surprise. You were conceived and born naturally and were so full of life right from the start. As you can see, boys, the world is a place of possibilities.

Life has many ups and downs and when you were both very young, mummy got critically ill and was in and out of hospital. You were too young to understand what was going on. Despite being told my chances of surviving were not great, I decided that I was going to live, to enjoy life to the fullest, to see you grow up and travel the world together to experience all its beauty.

You were my reason for battling on and for making a

full recovery. Our mind has incredible power, and we are capable of so much more than we give ourselves credit for.

Life is beautiful yet testing at the same time. Sometimes we are challenged beyond our wildest dreams, but always remember, the world is a place of endless possibilities and you can achieve anything you want to, if only you believe.

Maria Honeker is a holistic health mentor, motivational speaker and lover of plant-based foods. Born and raised in Sweden, she now lives in Somerset, UK, with her husband and two sons. A cancer survivor, her life mission is to empower others to overcome disease and achieve health and optimal well-being.

Remember the Power of Dressing

Lindsay Edwards

"Who do you want to be today?" I asked. Your eyes began to shine as you opened up the lid to your dressing up box, revealing the magical contents lying within. Your hands hovered above the cowboy bandana, superhero cape and wizard's wand as you considered my question. Your dressing up box led to a world of possibilities, one where you could be anything you wanted to be. The very moment you put on a costume you were instantly transported on a journey where you became the hero of your own imagination.

Like you, I had a dressing up box as a child too. Mine was filled with satin ribbons, beaded necklaces and beautiful dresses. When I wore my costumes, I became a fearless heroine on wild adventures in faraway lands.

Then one day, without knowing why, we wear a costume for the last time and close the lid of our dressing up box.

And with that, a part of our childhood ends.

We no longer ask ourselves, "Who do I want to be today?"

Now, I'm not suggesting for one moment that grown-ups ought go about their business wearing fancy dress costumes. Imagine if police officers dressed up as cowboys, teachers wore superhero capes and doctors waved magic wands! It would be rather difficult to take them seriously. Wouldn't it? But the magical effect of transforming yourself through the power of clothes needn't remain locked away within a dressing up box.

You have grown up watching me, as a Personal Stylist, greeting my clients at our door. Clients who you then see leaving, a few hours later, with an undeniable spring in their step. You see, my job as a Personal Stylist is not just showing my clients how to look good, it's showing them how to identify those clothes that make them feel incredible too.

How do I do this? I show them how to wear colour.

Wearing colour is one of the most powerful, yet simple, ways to positively influence our mood – and the mood of those surrounding us.

From now on, when you open your wardrobe doors each morning, I want you to ask yourself the following question: "How do I want to feel today?"

Now, pick your outfit carefully because the

psychological effects of wearing colour is remarkable.

Do you want to feel strong, powerful and confident? Then wear red to unlock those feelings within you.

When you want to feel calm, steady and relaxed, take some deep breaths and choose a blue or white outfit.

Wear green to feel revitalised and restore feelings of balance and harmony.

Do you want to feel sociable, energised and approachable? Then opt for orange.

Wear purple to evoke feelings of creativity, ambition and faith.

Yellow is known to be the happiest of all the colours. It will never fail to brighten your day and lift the spirits of those around you.

I want you to remember that all of the heroic qualities you will ever need in life are already inside of you. But on those days you doubt this, you know which colours to wear to remind you.

Love always,

Mum x

Lindsay Edwards is on a mission to make the world more colourful – one wardrobe at a time! She is the owner of REIMAGISE Personal Styling, providing a variety of transformative sessions to those looking to boost their image and confidence. Lindsay lives in Bedfordshire with her husband Ryan and their two sons Jake and Christopher.

Face Your Fear and Be Courageous

Sarah Burgin

I am yet to find my way; this does not mean I am broken or that I have failed.

My inner world is a tempestuous one. I have a constant, exhausting battle with the voice of self-doubt, it questions and analyses everything I say and do and picks apart even the most joyous of moments. I am unable to acknowledge any success as my own yet mistakes I own with passion. It has withdrawn me from human connections, it has stopped me using my fire for good, for speaking out and being the force I know I can be. It is also somewhat of a secret; I fear negative responses, so I keep it locked away inside, just for me.

I don't know when I shall find my way, but I remember the journey. I still feel the pain and frustration of dismissal, negated feelings and dreams, admonishment for mistakes, being woefully misunderstood, being criticised for who I am, but most of all, not having someone believe in me and stand by me. This then became my narrative of fear, self-loathing and shame.

Your father is the first experience I have had of unconditional love and support. He opened my eyes to my strengths. Then, along came motherhood – a new identity. A whirlwind of fear, self-doubt and a love so fierce it takes my breath away.

To know that my pain has the potential to taint the innocent perfection of our creation is paralysing. Then there are moments I want to run, I feel like my hurt stands to damage you and cause the exact thing I want to help you avoid. However, there is something I do know. There is somewhere self-doubt cannot creep, it cannot cause me to withdraw or run away, because this is for you both.

There is something I need you to know, my little ones: what you want in life, how you think, who you are, the challenges you face – I will support you, I will encourage you, I will see you and I will hear you. I will stand by your side through the storms and the sunshine and bear no judgement, only love. An unconditional, unwavering love for you to lean on without fear.

So, this I need you to remember, always – never let someone steal your light. No one should cause you to withdraw a piece of you from the world, to feel enough shame to hide it deep down inside; it will always fight to return and cause you deep unrest. Build your positive narrative, it will be your armour. Choose to face fear, be courageous every day and know, wholeheartedly, that I will be there. Never forget that I will help you build that armour, and I will help you repair it if the time comes. I don't want you to battle the journey as I do, I want you to embrace it.

Sarah Burgin lives in Northwich, UK and is mum to Leo (5) and Elodie (2) and wife to the wonderful Tom. After working in IT for twenty years and being adamant she wouldn't sing a single nursey rhyme in public after her first child, she started Baby College Warrington and Widnes and now sings nursery rhymes in front of entire classes of people!

Find Magic in the Ordinary

Jin-Ju Jahns

I was always an avid reader. And in my heart of hearts, I had a secret wish (as I'm sure all children do) of opening a closet door to Narnia, or following the white rabbit to Wonderland, or adventuring with Alanna the Lioness, or discovering I could bring characters to life by reading aloud. Accompanying these wishes was the ability to find the positive and magic in the simplest things. With this ability I lived my dreams. At seventeen, I backpacked through Europe alone. I studied literature in a castle in the mountains of Italy, I worked for a professional horse rider in Germany. I had a fairy-tale wedding and became "mama" to two beautiful boys. Somewhere along the road of growing up I lost sight of the ability to find the magic. I became world weary and disheartened by the hate and the waste and the greediness in our world. I questioned if it was responsible to bring children into a world so corrupt and ugly. Some days I am drowning in the endless laundry, the monotony of life in a never-ending lockdown, the incessant chatter of a three-year-old. It is this same chatter that can shine a light through my storm clouds. This chatter that finds wonder in the cat walking by and calls "good morning" to the budding tulips, regardless of the time of day; this chatter reminds me of the magic in our lives. Bright eyes turn an ordinary umbrella into a watermill, a pile of grey rocks into locomotives and wagons ready for an adventure.

To my beautiful tenacious children,

Thank you for helping me see the magic in the world again. Thank you for the reminder that you don't have to backpack across a continent to travel, and that an open mind and heart can fill you with joy and laughter. I wish for you to always find wonder in our world, and should you ever lose sight of it in the process of growing up, listen to the chatter of a three-year-old and immerse yourself in the magical world they see. Stay curious and always find the humor in life.

Born and raised in Montana, Jin-Ju Jahns has spent the last ten years in Germany. She is an avid reader, outdoor enthusiast and mom of two. Currently she spends her days building rock trains, finding new adventures with her boys in the Bavarian countryside.

Take a Chance on Yourself

Claire Chircop

I've never been a big believer in myself. As someone who's been deeply introverted, I feel like I've often been told what I could and couldn't achieve. These feelings have been around since I was in primary school, which now as a thirty-year-old woman fills me with such embarrassment. These feelings have dictated the vast majority of my life, made me doubt myself and my abilities and stopped me from striving for what could have been.

I didn't believe in myself.

I never took a chance on myself.

I wasn't living my life to its fullest potential.

Becoming a mother changed me! It brought eye bags and sleepless nights, but it also brought unexpected confidence. I didn't realise at first, but over the last two years I have transformed myself. When we become mums, we often lose so much of ourselves. We so rightly give so much of ourselves to our babies that we forget who we are as people and the passions we have. I went through this turmoil! I know those feelings, I've felt that negativity, but I'm out of the other side now.

I have a new mindset.

I'm now believing in myself.

I want my daughter to feel the same.

For me to be the best mother I can be to my daughter, I need to show her that I can be the best version of myself. I need to show her that I'm following my passions, believing in my abilities and taking a chance on myself. I want the belief I now have in myself to project onto my daughter... And that's what I'm doing.

I'm leading by example.

I'm projecting confidence.

I'm taking a chance on myself.

I recently did something that I've been wanting to do for a long time. I've weighed it up for such a long time. It's something that's scared me, but something that I knew I needed to do to live my life being the best version of myself... For me, my husband and my daughter!

I quit a job I was stuck in a rut with.

I quit a job that was making me feel unhappy.

I quit a job to follow my dreams.

I took a chance on myself! I quit a stable job in the middle of a pandemic to follow my dreams of becoming a freelance writer. With the help of my husband who has always believed in me more than I have myself, I made the jump and decided to completely turn my life around into one that I could be proud of. I now have a life which fulfils me and lets me be exactly who I want to be. And that is my only dream for my daughter.

I want my daughter to feel confident.

I want my daughter to believe in herself.

I want my daughter to feel like she can take a chance on herself.

Amelia-May, I want you to live the life you want to live, believing in yourself wholeheartedly and forever taking those chances!

Claire Chircop is a parenting blogger and mum of one, with another on the way, from the North East of England. She is an advocate of giving mum guilt the middle finger and showing empowerment in motherhood, whilst bringing mothers together through her 'Together In Mamahood' community.

Your Body Is Perfectly Wonderful, Just the Way It Is

Norma Thallon

I felt the familiar tug at my trouser leg. "Mummy?"

I looked down at my two-year-old daughter, who was staring back up at me.

"Mummy? Why you do your exercises?"

I had been setting up my home workout area (basically a mat and a kettlebell), which is presumably why she was asking me this pertinent question. As I looked down at her little face, I knew that it had already started. The watching. The mimicking. The learning. What I said to her now would lay the foundations for her own relationship with her body.

I have spent my entire life wishing for a smaller body.

I was about ten years old when I read a novel about a child who was being bullied at school because she was carrying more body fat than the other children. The character embarked on a secret exercise regime until she was the desired shape, when she 'unveiled' her new self to her peers in figure-hugging clothing, to great congratulation and celebration. The child was no longer bullied and lived happily ever after.

When I was twenty-four years old, I embarked on my own exercise regime. It wasn't secret, and there was no grand unveiling of a new body shape. But I did lose weight.

And then the compliments started. Family. Friends. Colleagues. All telling me how good I looked and asking how I had achieved such a transformation. What I had always suspected was confirmed – a body (my body) was more worthy when it was slim.

And so began my relationship with trading calories burned for calories eaten. Trying to be smaller. Leaner. Smoother. If I didn't make it to the gym, I felt guilty. If I ate something 'calorific' like chocolate and I hadn't been to the gym (and sometimes even if I had), I felt guilty. I hadn't earned it.

It was some time in between my first and second pregnancies that a shift occurred. I realised that I didn't want my entire life's work to be the pursuit of a smaller body. I wanted to be happy with the body I had then. With the body I have now. I finally began to view exercise as a way to nourish my body, not punish it. I stopped placing value judgements on foods – they were no longer 'good' or 'bad'. Just nutrient dense, or less so. Food doesn't need to be worked off. Treats don't need to be earned.

I want my children to know this, too. To know that they are more than their bodies. To see their bodies as amazing vessels that carry them through their lives. Bodies that don't need to fit into some socially constructed ideal. Bodies that are perfectly wonderful, just the way they are.

And so, as I looked down at my two-year-old daughter, who was looking back up at me with her enquiring eyes, I knew I could now tell her the truth. "I do my exercises to help me become stronger and stay healthy as I get older. Mummy wants to have a strong body, so she can play with you for a long time."

She laughed and nodded. "Yes. Good idea, Mumma, thumbs up."

Norma Thallon lives in Scotland with her partner Alec, two children Aimie (5) and Dylan (3) and two cats Smokie (6) and Skye (6). She runs her business Nurture Fitness from home and when she's not designing workouts for busy mums, she can be found baking banana bread, walking around her neighbourhood listening to audiobooks or trying to explain why "seventy a hundred six" isn't an actual number.

Turn Your Good Luck into a Gift for Others

Angharad Davies

He looked at me with wide incredulous eyes. Then the smile. Brighter than I had ever seen before. It was him just as he had ever been. His little swollen face couldn't hide his total surprise nor could his slow and gentle movements hide his excitement. He couldn't rush up to me or jump up and down on his bed. But I could see he was dancing behind those big brown eyes.

Mine was a fleeting visit today, not like those long summer days we spent in the hospital playroom just four months previously. We didn't share the same language – my Romanian was 'survival' – but we seemed to get on just fine. I remember one word still to this day, almost eighteen years on: "galben", which means yellow. It was his way of telling me he wanted to play with this yellow-backed domino set I had brought with me from back home to entertain the kids with.

But today was different. He was different. His prognosis was different. I gave him his Christmas present and watched him watch me. I had kept my promise of coming back soon. I wonder if he had understood me or even believed me when we said our goodbyes at the end of my two months of volunteering during university holidays.

I tried my hardest to push down the burning knot in my throat and to hold back the river of tears that were welling. I knew that the floodgates wouldn't hold, so I quietly slipped away while the nursing staff *ooohed* and *aaahed* as his hands slowly unwrapped the colourful Christmas paper.

I wish I could remember how we said our final goodbye. But I don't. Maybe it has faded with time. Maybe it's my way of swallowing the sorrow.

But I do remember our new hello.

As I walked down the busy streets of Bucharest that bleak December morning, I felt a cold tickle on my nose. I looked up at the grey covered sky and saw the tiny delicate sparkle of pure white snow. Each flake totally unique and unrepeated like a fingerprint from heaven. Each shimmer a reminder of what's truly important. And each touch the beginning of what I'm here to do.

Snow isn't something I get to see that often where I've lived and travelled. So, I wear it round my neck – a single silver snowflake – handmade and one of a kind. Close to my heart it helps me remember and share the greatest of lessons that I have to give to my children, the world:

Know when you are lucky.
And turn that good luck into a gift for others.

Angharad Davies is mum to two boys under four and lives in Wales, UK. She's the founder of The Positive Motherhood Project™ and the brains behind this very book. Her tongue-twister of a name is pronounced a little like Anne Harrod (for the non-Welsh readers out there!). After almost two decades of stop-starting her dream to make a difference in the world, this time she believes that there is no end to what could come from what she has started.

Spread Your Wings, and Keep Home in Your Heart

Lucy Jayne

Our packed moving truck drives down the street into the horizon. I can feel a lump in my throat, and tears building in my eyes. Today is the day we are leaving England for our new life in Florida. But how can I leave a home that's been mine for thirty-six years? I stand inside our empty house, so many special memories filling my head; how did I end up here?

I think back to March 2001, I'm nineteen years old, standing at Heathrow Airport with my friend. We are about to embark on a nine-month trip around the world. Our parents look emotional but they wave us off with proud smiles on their faces. I remember the words my mum said to me: "If it doesn't work out, you can always come home." I hold this thought in my heart, and it gives me great strength to grab this opportunity with both hands. Our first destination is Hong Kong. It's loud and bright, a mixture of futuristic skyscrapers and busy night markets, the streets filled with delicious mouthwatering food. Next is the beach paradise of Bali, Indonesia; rice paddies, beautiful temples and riding elephants in the jungle were just some of the highlights.

Of all the moments I experienced whilst travelling in 2001, my favourite one was meeting my husband in Perth, Australia. Who would've thought an American boy and an English girl could find each other on the other side of the world? I remember the day clearly; my husband approached us asking for advice, and we laughed, explaining we were not local. We continued to talk about our travels, including our upcoming stops in America. My husband's eyes twinkled, he smiled and said, "Of all the places in America, you are going to Seattle – that's where I'm from!" In that moment, I felt like us meeting wasn't an accident. I thought *this is going to be something*! And something it was... Two years later, he moved his whole life to England for me, in 2008 we got married, in 2010 and 2012 we welcomed our children, and in 2017 we all moved our whole life to Florida, to start a new adventure.

My hope for my own children is they will listen to their parents' adventurous story, and be inspired to explore this beautiful world. Life is full of crossroads, it is up to you which direction you head in. No risk is ever wasted, every step we take leads us closer to the person we are meant to be. The bold choices I made in 2001 led me to the life

I have now, a life I never thought would be mine; in my heart, I'm exactly where I'm meant to be.

"Take a leap of faith my beautiful children, you are loved and treasured, enjoy this world of possibilities, but remember if you carry home in your heart, you will never go wrong."

Lucy Jayne is mum to two amazing children, who are her proudest achievement. Born and raised in England, she now calls Florida home with her amazing husband, children and their dog Rosie. She loves travelling, photography, writing and biking. Approaching the age of forty in 2021, Lucy is taking on new challenges like cycling 3,000 miles in a year for the charity MND, and fulfilling her dream of writing a book.

You Have the Power to Break the Pattern

Tammy Rolfe

It was 2.37pm in the afternoon and my siblings and I were all called downstairs. I remember feeling very excited; there was a sense of anticipation in the air. We squashed in on the sofa, with me sitting next to my dad – I was a daddy's girl back then – and we waited eagerly to hear the news. Then like a tornado swooping in to rip my world apart, I was told, "Dad's moving out." At the age of ten, my life fell apart at the seams.

I'd seen a suitcase by the front door and just assumed it was all part of the surprise; little did I know it was my last time being a daddy's girl.

From that day on, the world changed dramatically for me. Not because my dad left, but the rejection I felt when he chose not to see us. That teamed with hearing my mum's account of the situation meant I could only interpret it to mean one thing: I was not loved, I was not worth visiting, I was not good enough.

I know now that both my parents were doing the best they could, but now having my own daughters with my own failed marriage, I was not about to sit back and let my children feel the rejection and lack of love that I had experienced growing up.

In life you have choices; you can follow the path that has been most trod or create your own path. This is not easy, but nor is feeling unloved, unwanted and unworthy.

If I can pass on a valuable piece of advice to my girls, it would be: 'Always know that you are in control of your life. You may not be in control of external factors, but you always have control over how you react to those situations, and the behaviour you adopt when they happen.

When your dad left when you were two and five, again, I felt like I had the rug pulled out from under my feet, my life was ripped apart at the seams! Luckily for you, I had already decided that I would not let my past experience be your experience.

I made the decision to act differently, and that is what I would like to pass down to you, you have the choice to act differently.

You have the choice to make the decisions that are positive for your life. Even though your dad left the family home, he did not leave you. I worked extremely hard under very difficult circumstances to ensure that you both felt loved, wanted and valued. There were many times when it was not easy, as emotions get in the way, things slipped out, and I'm not saying I was a saint, but I tried every day to put my autopilot on hold and actively break the patterns that had been embedded in me as a child, so that you could grow up with respect for men, and knowing you were loved.

Whatever life throws at you, and let's be fair life can through some big monkey poo sometimes, please just know that you always have choices, you can always be in control of your behaviour, and you can always choose to break the pattern.'

You've got this!

Award-winning coach, author, trainer and mum! Born in England, Tammy was diagnosed with social phobia at seventeen, a single mum of two by twenty-four, and spent a lifetime struggling with her mental health. Needless to say, she is extremely proud of the patterns she has broken to be able to achieve her goals! With a message to her mums, 'Be the Person You Want Your Child to Be', she now lives her life by the advice she would love to give her children, if only they would listen!

Everything You Need Is Already Inside You

Jo Ann Kobuke

At first, my fingers wouldn't cooperate. When they finally started to type, the words came out stilted and preachy. That's not what I wanted.

Heaven knows you've sat through enough of my rantings and ravings about why you shouldn't listen to songs that degrade women or why you must always stay true to your principles even though it's not convenient – especially when it's not convenient.

You've already soaked up as much of that as you're going to. The time for that has passed.

Now it's time to let you know you're ready. Ready to fly. I know it feels scary. It's natural to put it off, searching for that one last thing you think you need. But there is no one last thing.

When you were young, I'd have to give you a nudge – okay, sometimes a boot – in the behind to get you to flap your wings and try new things. It wasn't easy. You thought I was bossy and mean, but I know you realize now the value in those experiences.

Remember this when you're struggling to get your child to expand their horizons, think of me when they're glaring at you, with their sullen face, body stiff, arms crossed. You can get through it, just as I did, and you'll be rewarded with a strong and confident adult, just as I have been, so hang in there.

I won't lie, it was hard to see you struggle and even harder to see you hurt or have you angry at me. I had to remind myself it wasn't my job to protect you from life; it was my job to prepare you for life. I had to accept there would be tears, yours and sometimes mine.

Shielding either of us from those tears would have kept you from becoming the resilient, self-reliant, and independent thinker you are today. When you're a mother, being the bad guy comes with the territory. It's something I had to endure so you could learn to embrace life, bumps and all.

Often, I struggled to find the right balance between giving you enough freedom to develop your skills and confidence and creating a safe environment in which to do that. I didn't always get it right, as you, the cheeky teenager, would often remind me. But I did the best I could, which is all a mother can ever do.

Motherhood pushed all my buttons, or rather, you

pushed them all – over and over as you explored where the boundaries were and why they existed. What kept me sane was reminding myself why I was torturing us both.

It was all to help you become the woman you are today. A wise and compassionate woman capable of tackling anything. A woman determined to do all she can in and for the world.

It's so easy to doubt ourselves and lose track of who we are, blinded by the shiny objects life dangles before us. My job now is to hold up the mirror when doubts creep in and remind you of the amazing human you are.

And when time has its way, and I am no longer here in this physical body, know that my spirit will remain to remind you of who you are and the love we share.

Jo Ann Kobuke is the mother of two adult daughters. She lives on the west coast of the US with her husband and dog. After retiring as a CPA in the not-for-profit world, she began a second career coaching women as they navigate the ups and downs of midlife. You can find her community, the Messy Midlife Society, on Facebook. She loves traveling, eating out, plays, spending time with family, and life in general.

Be Kind

Kate Taylor

When I was just twenty-three years old, I made a huge life decision to walk away from the religion that I was raised in. Everyone I had ever known turned their backs on me because of that decision and so my life started again. The only person I had that day was your dad (Uncle Matt was in Australia travelling at the time).

I could have gone on to have a life feeling very bitter and angry, cross with everyone and feeling resentful, but I was determined from that point to be very aware of how I treat others.

You know that I always try to be kind, I try never to judge people, and I am always ready to listen. You don't know what life experiences someone has had, you don't know what they go home to each day, you don't know what they may be hiding, so always be kind. You simply don't know the impact a few kind words could have on someone's day.

Educate yourself on other people's beliefs, don't be ignorant and assume that what you believe is the only way and because someone else's belief is different it must be wrong. Of course, discuss beliefs, listen, learn, debate but don't judge. I think of the saying "variety is the spice of life" and I am proud of how open I am to other people's choices now, and I see that openness in you because that's all I have ever taught you.

Remember too how strong you are. I know you are strong because I have watched you. I have watched you carry on going to school when I know it was the last place you wanted to be sometimes. I've seen you struggling mentally, working out what you want, what you need but being able to come and talk to me. I have heard how you have described helping your friends when they have been struggling and you have been such a lovely supportive friend back to them despite how you were feeling.

I think my hypnotherapy was part of this journey that eventually made me realise I could do something with my kindness and how I love to support people. I was really determined to study hard and turn it into a business even though I had another job and the house to sort out. I hope it showed you that if you really want something and you can work hard, then go for it, it's completely possible.

Be kind, don't judge, explore the world, do things that make you happy.

x

Kate is a clinical solution focused hypnotherapist based in Bristol, UK. Kate has two teenagers, two pugs and just the one husband. She enjoys hosting friends at her lovely home and discovering new places to eat and drink around the beautiful Bristol Harbourside.

All We Have Is Now

Priya Logan

When I became pregnant for the first time, it felt like the unfolding of a promise of life. There was something in the hope of a new heartbeat nestled deep within my expanding tummy that took away what was a few years of loss and grief within the family. Pregnancy was challenging at times but filled with a sense of purpose and clarity.

When you were born, I was shocked by the sense of fragility and protectiveness I felt about you and the world. I couldn't watch the news or think of anything violent. Everything was cocoon soft, precious, irreplaceable. When you had a health scare at four weeks old, I cried for three hours straight. Everything turned out fine, yet I was aware that this was a signal that motherhood had changed me, as my life became so intimately connected with another human's well-being.

I lost my grandfather on the other side of the world when you were not even six months old. The loss was visceral, tangible and I leant ever more into your radiant smile, plump cheeks and the perpetual newness of your every encounter with the expanding world.

I was at times a planet in orbit of your sunlight and counted on your progressions to mark mine. I read every book on development and the next steps, always tracing a path in the unknown but perfect family future.

When you were not quite three, I became pregnant again. We also went through a flurry of financial crises, each more intense than the last. It overwhelmed us as a family and left us on the brink of bankruptcy and stress. Just after I gave birth to your brother, we had another big move. You were three and a half. You had been struggling with tiredness and thirst, but I kept putting it down to having a few runs of antibiotics.

Eventually, we sought advice; the blood test was all it took to tell us that you had type 1 diabetes. It was a shock. The management of diabetes is relentless and harsh. First, we all found it debilitating, but it threw what was valuable into sharp focus again. We were overwhelmed with the positive support through the health board and with others.

That was thirteen years ago this year. Although no one would choose it, having a significant condition like diabetes in your life forces you to slow down, put things in perspective and count your blessings when you are fortunate enough to receive health care and support. Having someone you love and cherish in all their uniqueness means taking a more challenging road becomes a willing sacrifice and puts more surmountable problems into the background. I love you, Rhiannon, and thank you for teaching me patience, perseverance and the preciousness of now.

Priya is a garden lover, sporadic artist and mother of three perpetually growing children. Living by the North Sea in Scotland in the astringent Northern wind, she loves connecting with people, plants and pottering with discarded objects.

Follow Your Dreams – and Look for the Rainbow!

Sophie Price

Barnaby,

Whenever you feel as though you are on the wrong path, just look for the rainbow to guide you. Rainbows can appear even in the darkest of times and just that sparkle of light is enough to keep you going for one more day.

One of the hardest journeys I have ever been on was the road to becoming a drama teacher. This lifelong dream which seemed so certain suddenly became so difficult. There were many times at the start of my journey when I felt like giving up. Every day I called your nanny and grandad to ask them to bring me home and, every day, they asked me to try for one more day. If I still felt the same the next day, they would come to get me. This conversation continued for quite a few weeks until, eventually, I got through it. At the end of the journey, I had completed my training and had achieved my goal. There were times when I didn't think I could do it, but your grandparents showed me the way. They were my rainbow.

This is my advice to you. There will be times in your life when you wonder if you should give up. There will be times when you just want to go home. That is exactly when you need to dig deep – maybe your rainbow will be in the sky, or maybe it will be in your dreams, maybe in the eyes of Mummy or Daddy. There will always be a rainbow to guide you and show you that there will always be light. You can achieve anything as long as you believe in yourself. The whole world is at your feet – and those feet can take you wherever you want to go.

Sometimes the road can be long, but you might find that you learn new things about yourself along the way. And just like another ('yellow brick') road we both love, you might even make some very special friends along the way who, just like you, are searching for their very own rainbows.

I want you to believe, my darling, that anything is possible when you follow your dreams, as long as you trust your brain, follow your heart and have the courage to look for the rainbow and keep going – just for one more day.

All roads will always lead you to home, where Mummy and Daddy will be. And we all know, 'there's no place like home'.

Love,

Mummy

Sophie Price lives in Berkshire with her husband Tom and gorgeous baby boy, Barnaby. Becoming a mummy in 2020 was the most special role for this drama teacher. Sophie loves to put on shows with Barnaby at home – his most prestigious role being the Cowardly Lion from The Wizard of Oz (if only he could remember his lines!). She is currently building her Sophie Price Hypnotherapy business, following new dreams and rainbows.

You Have All the Tools You Need Within You to Create a Happy, Confident Life

Saffron Cooksey

No matter how tough things get, I very much want you to know that there are always positive solutions. As a child and teen, I suffered with a number of anxiety-related issues including selective mutism, social anxiety, generalised anxiety, insomnia and various phobias (including an intense fear of dogs, spiders, lifts, escalators and deep water). It overwhelmed me to the extent that I had few friends and rarely left my bedroom for the first twenty years of my life. This feeling of powerlessness led to bouts of depression, although at the time I didn't understand that the oppressive waves of sadness I experienced were actually depression.

I was fortunate that there was one thing I knew I could

do well and that was to be a learner. I threw myself into my education as I realised that this was my escape route out of my learned helplessness. However, I didn't enjoy school, not even in the slightest. In fact, as with many anxiety sufferers, school felt like a highly toxic environment to me, and I literally had to drag myself there every day.

I was a highly sensitive person with low self-esteem and, as such, teacher feedback sent my meerkat into overdrive and I viewed it as negative criticism. I've since learned to appreciate feedback and I hope you'll do the same as it gives us a valuable opportunity to improve. Like you, I was a quiet and cooperative child and, as such, my difficulties went unnoticed and untreated.

When I passed my exams, I felt there was only one path I could possibly take and that was to go to university. Secretly, I chose this route because the thought of having to find a job absolutely terrified me, but conversely the thought of continuing to stay in my room alone, lonely and unemployed, filled me with crushing fear and panic. For the whole of the first term of university, I genuinely don't think I uttered one word to anyone. I had reached an all-time low!

Please never be afraid to fall because, when you reach your lowest point, that is your turning point. I was desperate to find answers! I did a whole lot of soul searching and came to realisations that completely changed my life. These are the messages I want to share with you: Always know that your mind is extremely powerful, and you actually have all the tools within you to create a happy and fulfilled life.

No one else can change your life for you. Only you can do that.

And, above all, remember to embrace the bumps along the road. See them as a chance to learn and grow and this way you will discover how to navigate them confidently and consistently.

Saffron is a mum of two amazing teens – a fifteen-year-old son and a thirteen-year-old daughter, not forgetting her three fur babies who bring so much fun and laughter into her family. She is happily married and lives in Cardiff, UK. She is an award-winning online emotional resilience coach who is passionate about empowering young people and parents to achieve confidence, resilience and happiness. She is a keen reader and loves spending time in nature and socialising with friends.

Don't Have Regrets

Sarah Simpson

I don't regret my competitive nature. I like to win. Whether it be a card game against my brother, back in school where there was friendly competition between my best friend and I to see who got the higher marks, or even just trying to get more heart points when my husband and I work out together. I love it.

I don't regret being bossy. It's just me. I like to tell people what to do. I like to organise everything, and I like to bring everyone together. As a teenager when we went on girls' holidays, I was always the friend telling everyone that their insurance didn't cover jet ski rides. Every group of friends needs the bossy one with a big heart.

I don't regret doing a degree that I didn't use. How many eighteen-year-olds know what they want to be when they grow up? Seriously, how many thirty-year-olds do? I did what I was good at and what I thought I would enjoy. Living by yourself, learning that there's such a thing as a white and dark wash (I was far too spoilt growing up) and making some of the best friends, who still to this day open new doors up to me, was the best experience ever.

I don't regret not going travelling. I loved my twenties. Buying my first house was epic. Why would I have wanted to decide on a capsule wardrobe to fit into a backpack when I could fill a double (much to my boyfriend's, now husband's dismay) with all my clothes? Decorating the house together, saving to buy beautiful furniture and having dinner parties with friends was just perfect to me.

I don't regret leaving teaching. When I became a teacher, I wanted it all. My plan was to move through the ranks and I made the move to a school where fast progression was an option. What I didn't know on the day that I accepted the job was that I was pregnant. Who knew that a tiny little human could make you rethink your entire life plan? Instead of going for head of department, I went for head lady who lunches and only returned to work three days. This worked for our family with two children. Luckily for me, after the twins' arrival when we became a family of six, a fantastic opportunity landed on my lap that meant I could work, engage my brain and be a full-time mammy; success gained a whole new meaning to me.

I don't regret having four children. The more the merrier! Finding out we were having twins did make me rethink hand-me-down acceptances, but it was like winning the lottery. To have four healthy, happy children is the dream. It was actually a joke amongst friends that we would end up having twins when I fell pregnant for the third time. For the people that say 'double trouble', I say 'double the fun!' My children are my biggest accomplishment.

Everyone has things in their lives that they would have done differently, hindsight is definitely a wonderful thing. But my message to you, my darling four, is this: be you. Own your decisions, be proud of the person you are and don't regret a thing.

Sarah Simpson lives in the North-East of England with her husband, four children Nellie (8), Sammy (6), twins Roscoe and Trixie (3) and not forgetting her Yorkie, Delia. She is an ex-teacher and now runs a successful online business FM Fragrances by Sas and coaches a team of over 1000 people.

Be Courageous and Trust Your Inner Voice to Guide you

Charlotte-Louise Clarke

Before I became a mother, I had always been determined and headstrong, particularly in my career. I've had my fair share of knockbacks and heartbreaks like most, but I have learned how to be resilient, dust myself off and get back up. These traits have proven useful in motherhood so far for raising my child but it's only now that I reflect upon where or how I may have gained them. I realise that both my grandmother and mother instilled in me this set of disciplines without even realising, and my life experiences have proved what a valuable gift it is.

My grandmother was the matriarch of our family; if anyone needed advice or to be rescued from an injustice, she was there. People drew on her strength, kindness and compassion. At the same time, she was a no-nonsense woman and was an excellent judge of character.

Strength, kindness and compassion were traits she passed to my mother who, from a young age, I watched being put through a needlessly messy divorce with my father, a man truly the opposite to my mother in every possible way. Through the struggle, she raised me to be the best possible version of myself. She taught me life lessons that have always served me well, such as you can have anything you want in life when you work hard for it, and you should never feel you have to be in a relationship with someone because you need them, but because you love and want to be with them.

I have learned that I am a descendent in a line of fierce women, women who are empowered by the experiences that have shaped who they are. My daughter is a continuation of this line of fierce women. She too is determined and headstrong. This is something I hope she will continue to be despite my feelings on a school morning when her fashion choices are not quite what her school would call uniform, or when she goes at her own pace though life, believing the world will wait for her, when I am rushing to get her to school on time.

Nevertheless, I hope she isn't afraid to be the one that stands out for her courage, standing up for the things that matter to her. That she isn't afraid to give up when things aren't going her way. That she sees failure as an opportunity to learn and grow and that in her darkest moments she finds strength. I hope she listens to her inner voice and trusts it to take her where she needs to go.

Charly Clarke lives in Leicestershire in the UK with her five-year-old daughter Savannah. Charly has her own business supporting parents through antenatal care, infant massage and holistic therapy treatments. Of all her roles, she loves being a mum the most. Recently she has come to realise that, especially through a pandemic, strengthening skills such as cocktail making can prove very useful.

Don't Suffer in Silence

Donna Crighton

"What mental health needs is more sunlight, more candour, and more unashamed attention."

Glenn Close

As someone who has struggled with mental health in both my personal life and from seeing it as a registered mental health nurse in my professional life, I would like my daughter to know that it is more than 'okay to not be okay', as the saying goes. In my personal life I have previously felt shame about my battle with anxiety and depression. Most notably after I had an emergency c-section at thirty-three weeks and my daughter was admitted to the neonatal unit where she stayed for four weeks.

At the start I tried to 'put on a brave face', as they say, and after a week of trying to do this I broke down in the ward after a nurse had shown concern for me. Once I opened myself up to the nurses, I got the help that I very much needed and so started my path to mental health recovery.

I had experienced birth trauma and post-natal depression, which I am still battling with. I tried my hardest to put on a brave face until one day I broke and realised I was drowning. I needed to face up to the fact that I needed help, which was no easy thing to admit. But the only way to eradicate the stigma associated with mental health is to fight it head on and to speak openly about it.

My experiences have really shaped my belief in highlighting the importance of educating children on mental health and the prejudices that surround it. Children are the future, and I would like my daughter to know how hurtful taunts and terms such as 'nutcase' can be. They can have an impact on someone and it continues to fuel the judgement faced by those who experience mental health problems.

The main message I would like to convey to my daughter is that there is no shame in being mentally unwell and to battle it you need support behind you. I have seen the devastating effects suicide can have in both my personal and professional life, hence why I place so much importance on creating a world where people don't fear being stigmatised for being mentally unwell.

I feel this would really benefit my daughter as no one is immune to mental health problems and I want to create an open and honest environment where she can discuss her feelings openly, therefore allowing her to maintain her confidence and self-esteem. I never want her to feel ashamed of who she is.

There are too many people who view talking about mental health as a weakness. Too many people trying to put on a brave face. I learned that mental health problems don't go away by themselves and are certainly not a sign of weakness. Let me tell you something, my dear, asking for help is one of the bravest steps of all.

Donna Crighton is the mother of a girl called Matilda. She is a mental health nurse. She got married in New York City. Born and raised in Aberdeen, Scotland. Mother to a premature baby, she has detailed her life as a mother in her Facebook blog 'Preemie Mama Drama'.

Trust Who You Are, Be Bold with Your Character!

Katherine Mackness

It was a few days after having my son, I looked down at my chapped nipples, and I was thinking could I carry on breastfeeding? It was something I loved doing but was it worth the pain? I now know this is my metaphor for life. Sometimes life deals you cracks, usually full of shit, but over time, with persistence and trusting your own gut, it will heal and become a smoother ride. Learning those self-care strategies enable us to stop the cracks appearing on the nipple in the first place, or needing those self-healing techniques.

I count my lucky stars I have a strong influence in my mum, as well as my loopiness from her too (would be so boring to be normal!), two supportive sisters (also loopy) and the 'Bromage' head thought from my dad "trust your gut". My dad and I have larger than average head size, thanks dad! Not medically proven, we have just gone off the size of the Christmas cracker hats! I say it's because we have masterful brains.

Even though I had to find this out for myself, those pre-nipple-cracking preventative techniques or self-healing skills didn't really start to resonate until I met my now husband (very much laid back, well strongly horizontal actually), who is an avid gut follower and my rock.

I am now a stronger individual and having my son has given me that extra strength to push and do what I believe to be right. Not what others make you believe is society's way of fitting in. The world would be boring if no one trusted their own thoughts and followed what we believe others think is normal, but I did it and I still question my actions now. But hell to it, what's good about having a gut if we don't listen to it when it gurgles! If someone doesn't like what you are, bugger to them, it's what you want to do and what you believe to be important and that's what matters. I want my son to trust his personality that he can do whatever he puts his mind to, and I want to reassure mums that you are worthy and your gut instincts matter and are usually pretty much right.

The more I think about trusting my instincts and believing in myself, the more I should follow from my son. The way he wants to explore the world through curiosity, showing stubbornness, following what he wants to do (usually being a dust collector on clothes shop floors, yes very much an avid crawler at the age of one!), but yes, I am going to make sure he does what he wants to do, and make sure he trusts his gut.

Stay strong; do not let the world dampen your big-headed loopy character! And if cracks do appear that's okay, because I am going to make sure you have learnt the ability to trust yourself to know that you can help heal them and move forward, becoming stronger, and to follow that gurgling gut (even if it means eating a large pepperoni pizza first). I persisted, I did what I thought was right and, for those that want to know, my breastfeeding journey continues. TRUST YOURSELF.

Katherine Mackness has a calming, quiet strength, with intent to nurture and care. First time mummy to a rambunctious rug-rat, wife to a full-hearted husband, fur baby mummy to their cat, Katherine lives with her family in the East Midlands, UK, and is an advocate for supporting children and their families professionally and personally, showering everything she does with care and love.

You Are Not Broken

Jo Broadey

Dear Julia,

What is the most important lesson I would like to teach you? Do not let others make you believe you need to be fixed. You were never broken to begin with.

Why am I telling you this? Because it is a lesson I have had to learn the hard and painful way. Growing up was not an easy process for me and there have been so many times where I have wished I could be someone different. You have inherited my quiet and introverted nature, and you may also sometimes feel the world is not made for people like us. These are the times when you will need to remember that you are here for a reason.

I will not lie to you, my darling girl, this life is hard. Periods of hope have been followed with periods of depression and self-harm. Returning home after university, I received job rejection after rejection and felt the constant sting of judgment from others around me. Thankfully, the universe sent me a life raft in the form of teaching, and I grasped it with both hands. But the feelings were only placed in storage.

After you were born, having endured months of sickness and the anxiety of a house move that seemed destined to never be completed, the lid of the box fell off. By the time you came along, my brain was in the perfect state for the seeds of depression to grow, and all it needed was a life-changing event to tip the scales. In those first few months of motherhood, I was so unwell I could not hold you, or even stand to be in the same room as you. But, gradually, the fog began to clear and I fell in love with you.

Sadly, despite the joy you bring me every day, I was doomed to repeat this experience with your brother. In some ways, the second fall was even harder than the first, and it cost me my job and career in classroom teaching. Another door closed in my face. As has happened to me so many times in my life, a period in the wilderness followed.

However, I am a firm believer that there is a plan for us. My second attempt at launching a business has been highly successful, and I am now in the process of growing a team. What do I want you to learn from this? That things do change, and the wheel always turns. There will be people who try to make you feel as if it is your fault when things do not work out. This is not true, and it has taken me thirty-four years to realise. Hopefully, if there is one gift I can give you, it is that you will not need to wait this long. The journey has been arduous and there is still a long way left to go. But, for the first time in my life, I have realised that I am not broken.

Jo Broadey is an English teacher and mum to two beautiful children, Julia, 5, and Peter, 3. She lives in Dartford, Kent and runs Bright Sky Tutoring, an English tutoring service. Jo is a keen reader, as well as an enthusiastic consumer of chocolate and white wine!

You Are MORE than Enough

Anupa Roper

She sat and looked in the mirror. There were big tears running down her face. Ever since she could remember, she had wasted so much time and energy feeling sad at the words and actions of others. Now, she was stronger. Now, she knew better. She knew that her worth was not based on the way that she looked on the outside; on the size of her 'skinny' legs. More importantly, she didn't ever want her children to grow up feeling the same.

That 'she' that I talk of isn't just a woman that I watch from the sidelines, a woman I can sympathise with but never really, truly understand her feelings. Because that woman is me. That 'she' is me. I finally know that I am loved, I am beautiful, I am worthy, I am more than enough. But there was a time when my appearance made me feel so unworthy. A time when I missed out on many wonderful experiences.

It began at school, age eleven, a time when others were growing into their bodies. Meanwhile, my body remained the same, my tiny legs and arms stood out. I felt so worried about how my legs looked to others that I would even wear two pairs of tights to bulk them out! I began to get teased. It's hard enough growing up, with insecurities and uncertainties about so many things. My self-esteem was nowhere to be found but not a single person would have known from the way that I behaved. How would they? I was the class clown; always making people laugh.

That has remained through the years, my outside persona never revealing the sadness inside. In fact, it only served to make everyone believe that I was super confident. So, when did I stop placing so much heartache on the girl in the mirror? I'm sad to say it was only as recently as the last few years. The saddest part is that I have missed out on loving myself. That was torn away from me at a young age. Slowly, I have realised that my beauty is so much more than my appearance. Slowly, I have learnt to love myself, every single part of me. I know that I am beautiful inside and out. Because I am me!

My arms and legs may be slender, but my heart is big. I have so much more to give to this world. So do you. We are all loved, we are all beautiful, we are all worthy, we are all more than enough.

So go... be brave, be real, be you!

Anupa Roper lives in Leicestershire, UK, with her husband and two children (Maya 11 and Ayden 10). She allowed her label of 'skinny' to hold her back, so now she is on a mission to support the next generations to know that they are more than enough just the way they are. You can find her as 'Sparrowlegs' on Instagram and Facebook and this is also the title of her debut children's book about a sparrow who learns to love the feathers she is in.

Setbacks are Opportunities in Disguise

Leeann Murphy

"Welcome to the world, my love," I said as I peered down into my newborn baby's squinting eyes. She was finding her sense of touch for the first time, curled up, skin-to-skin, on my chest.

"I guess we should cancel today's baby shower?" my mother said smiling.

My child's arrival was spontaneous and unexpected. She arrived four weeks early, and six hours before her baby shower – an event that was on, then off, then on again due to COVID-19.

Was I disappointed that my much longed-for baby shower didn't happen as expected?

Not one bit. My life expectations had rarely come to fruition.

In my twenties, in Australia, I expected I'd climb the corporate ladder, meet my Prince Charming and live the fairy tale I'd learnt about as a little girl: build a home, get married, start a family together.

Now, at the age of forty-three, I look at my daughter taking her first breaths and recall the life events that led to her arrival today.

My mind turned to my father who passed away when I was thirty-one. The setback of losing him and the enormity of grief I felt was the catalyst to change my life and live in Istanbul, honouring his life lesson.

'Life is too short to stay still too long,' he had taught me.

I decided to dismount that corporate climb and swapped my business heels for freelancing flip flops, travel writing across Turkey.

Life became good again.

Then in my mid-thirties, my life expectations came crashing down once more. I was ready to take the next step, in love with my 'tall, dark and handsome' partner in Turkey. Yet, the country was facing major dissent and I doubted I could have a long-term commitment to Turkey, and therefore my partner.

When he confessed, "I can't do this anymore," doubting our longevity too, the heartbreak eventually led me back to Australia to find the fairy tale I wanted to live.

As my daughter nuzzled under my chin, I thought of the times I tearfully faced my 'fortilities' – my fertile forties – one setback after another. I was single and wanting children. Freezing my eggs was a process I investigated but couldn't afford, nor one that guaranteed success. I continued to pray that my Prince Charming was one swipe away.

He wasn't.

At forty, I finally turned my back on the fairy tale finish and started the process to become a solo mother by choice, through IVF with the generosity of a donor. A process I had been considering for four years.

IVF was full of setbacks too. But I had learnt that, like a child needs to crawl before they can walk, or like a butterfly needs a cocoon before they can fly, every difficult, clumsy or painful moment faced was necessary for bigger and better things.

Expectations often lead to stress and disappointment but setbacks – they are opportunities in disguise! Opportunities where big life decisions were made, or major life lessons were learnt that led me to where I am today: completely in love and the happiest I've ever been!

I smiled at my daughter cooing in my arms. "You are my fairy tale finish, my princess, and we're going to live happily (and spontaneously) ever after together!"

Leeann Murphy has worn many hats over the years: project manager, travel writer, copywriter and belly dancer, though her most treasured role being a solo mother by choice. Leeann shares her biggest lesson in becoming a first-time mum in her forties for her daughter and other women seeking a similar path to motherhood.

By Dreaming, You Set Your Own Reality in Motion!!

Aarti Popat

Dreams are those sparks that help you to create a beautiful reality and you must always always dream. Sometimes those dreams are straightforward and you can achieve them as easily as I know you can my beautiful children… but others, they take hard work and determination!

The route to achieve them may not be easy or you might struggle, but I'd love you to know that there is a strategy that will get you there!

There is a way forward.

There is a way to get your dreams to become your reality.

And there is always a way to live the life that you want and be happy because the ultimate goal in life is to be happy!

When I was younger, I was inspired by creative spaces

and those programmes on television that talked about transforming your rooms and I found it fascinating. It hooked me – I loved it. I changed all of the rooms in the house, countless times, it was as if I had found my passion. I decided I wanted to 'be' an interior designer when I grew up!

I was so so excited; I was fifteen and I had decided what I wanted to be!! Oh my God!

I told everybody I would help everyone with their rooms and their homes from then on.

I also started to research interior designers, who they were and what they did, so that I could understand what I would need to do. I looked at the various education routes into the industry and eventually, one day, I knew I wanted my own business – to be my own boss!

After my research, I started to piece all the parts of the puzzle together because to achieve a goal you have to have a plan, a strategy – I knew where I wanted to be, I had to take the right steps to get there. By breaking it down, it made it all simple – I had a roadmap.

I went off to art school, I got my degree and I was excited, but the happiness was only elevated after I got my first job. It was an exhilarating feeling, knowing that this was something that I had wanted from the age of fifteen, and here I stood working at a design agency working on all things interiors!

It just goes to show – dream your dream, but don't leave it to stay a dream, make a plan to make it a reality – you can do it!!

BUT:

Remember, there will always be bumps on the road, it's how you plan to overcome them that is important. Your actions, your alterations to the plan to make it work – THIS is important!

Your life isn't a series of steps that follow a logical order... and that's okay, because sometimes you face obstacles in life, which you hadn't foreseen. Sometimes the path you take is longer, but you can do it.

Always do you in your own style, and you will get there, you will achieve!

So, my beautiful children, make sure you always dream and make sure you always plan to achieve those dreams.

Whatever you decide to dream and do – Mummy is always going to be proud of you and will always be here! Love you both lots and lots xx

Aarti Popat is a devoted mother to two beautiful children, 2 and 5. She lives in North-West London with her ever-supportive husband and two minis. She is an interior designer, consultant and mentor working in interiors for over fifteen years. As well as creating beautiful interiors she helps aspiring interior designers start up and follow their interiors passions and has founded Aarti Popat Interior Design and The Interior Designers Club – a community for ambitious female interior designers!

It Is Safe to Change Your Mind

Jo Tucker

I am one of those people who seems to change their mind a lot. Always learning something new and never content with just settling. If you are outside of my head my decisions often don't make sense, but to me the connections are obvious. And regardless of what others have said or may think, I always go for whatever feels good to me. There is so much evidence in my past proving that my decisions have been exactly what was needed for this present moment.

I hated school and I left as soon as possible, choosing to go to college, despite all of my friends staying to do A Levels. I started at a college that involved daily hour commutes on a train and then a bus five days a week, without a familiar face. I felt the odd one out for not wanting what my friends did and not choosing to follow them regardless of being different or risking losing our connection. The commute felt exciting, it was exhilarating having that level of freedom and time to myself, never feeling fazed about the prospect of something completely new and so completely independent. Three years later, I went to university, again away from anyone I knew, and proved I could get a degree in science (two actually), despite being told I wasn't academic and science wasn't my strong point. I was told I'd be shovelling s*** for the rest of my life if I wanted to work with animals. Of course, I found another way as an Environmental Specialist, which manifested itself despite not even applying for the job.

Finally, I felt I could have a baby, the thing I had desperately wanted for years. My mum told me that having a baby would hurt as soon as she heard the news. After a quick search on the internet, I found out that a calm positive birth was a thing and had an incredible birth experience because of it, again stepping outside of expectations. Then, unexpectedly, I decided I didn't want the career path I had chosen anymore. I retrained as a hypnobirthing teacher and doula, starting up my own business despite never doing anything like it before. By the time my second baby came along, I was the most well-prepared parent-to-be you could imagine!

Then it happened again, I decided I didn't want to do it anymore, closed my business and right now I am training as a Subconscious Transformation Coach and Shift Method Facilitator.

Sometimes I would wonder, what do other people think, am I being irresponsible? Most of the time these things happened without thinking being involved. What I do know is that every step has taught me exactly what I needed for this moment. My own mental health struggles have woven into each experience, preparing me for now. I learned to embrace my own authenticity and gained the confidence to live life as my uncensored self.

Don't ever be afraid to change your mind, always follow your instinct and trust that you cannot get it wrong.

Jo Tucker is quietly rebellious, a questioner of everything and her own best client. Raiser of two magical beings, on a mission to help other mums embrace their full uncensored selves, so that the next generations will benefit on a deeper level from these audacious change makers. She resides near Reading, UK.

Your Body Is Your Home, Trust in It

Kim Mousley

"You are doing it!"

This might be the point where I finally realised my body was actually much smarter than me. I was in the birth pool, moments from meeting you for the very first time, and all I could tell myself was, "I can't do this." Our midwife was fantastic: she had taken a back seat and let things unfurl with little assistance, but now she stepped in. "You are doing it!" Firm… but kind. I finally saw that my body was way more powerful than I had given it credit for. It was actually doing it!

I've spent many years berating my body. My criticisms wax and wane but have always been there in the background. Why isn't my tummy smaller? Why aren't my legs slimmer? I exercised to 'fix' my body. I was totally obsessive for a while. Unable to let go of the plan. Feeling guilty if I missed a workout. Eating less to balance it out. But 'happy' because I was in control.

I had grand plans for pregnancy. It wouldn't change me. I'd keep working out. I'd show everyone how strong I was. It turned out my body had different ideas for me!

Even a few days before I realised my period was a bit late, I was feeling nauseous. A reassuring early symptom turned out to be relentless. And the exhaustion was another level. One evening around just six weeks, I called your dad and said I was too tired for the gym. He encouraged me to go, knowing there would be an aftermath of guilt if I didn't, but I just burst into tears – I wasn't sure I could even stay awake to get there. What was happening to me? The first trimester wore on and I couldn't even compensate with healthy eating. All I could stomach was white toast. I waited eagerly for the magic twelve-week milestone when I would feel better and could get moving again but it never came. I felt like my body was betraying me.

After an episode of reduced movements in the second trimester, the midwife instructed me to call in to work sick for the remainder of the week, go home and just rest. As soon as I had permission to be still, you woke right up again, and all was fine.

My body had been calling to me with the sickness and exhaustion and I had continued to ignore it, creating my own stress about what I couldn't do anymore, rather than seeing the wonder it was already doing. You made me listen eventually and give my body what it needed. It could provide everything you needed – nourishment, shelter, love – but I had to slow down and get some perspective!

It's clear to me now, my body knew what it was doing all along. There was no need to tell it what to do, it just knew! There is some magical, innate wisdom there. The thought of you ever hating your beautiful body strikes sadness into my heart, so I hope that you realise what an incredible invention you have been gifted long before I did. For me, it's time to befriend my body again. It's my home.

Kim Mousley lives in Bristol, UK, with her husband and three-and-a-half-year-old daughter. Pregnancy did not suit her well and she met many challenges on her journey to motherhood. On her journey, pregnancy yoga and hypnobirthing transformed her perspective, so much so that she has since become a pregnancy yoga teacher herself and finds great happiness in supporting mums in their journey to parenthood.

To Thrive in Life, Keep an Open Mind and Adjust to Circumstances!

Valerie Navarro

For as long as I can remember, I always heard French people were terrible at learning foreign languages. Every single year, French media would tell us, graphs in hand, how bad we were compared to the rest of the world. At school, I "learned" English, German, Spanish, Latin, Portuguese and Russian. Of course, with such a mindset imposed on me, I had terrible grades, mostly because I couldn't see why I should waste time on subjects I was 100% sure to fail.

My parents sent me to England for one month when I was fourteen, to improve my (very bad) English. We were forty French teenagers, away from home for the first time. Of course, my English was as bad as before when I came back home, and I got into trouble. I had, then, this bright idea: later on, I will marry an English man, so that my kids will not have to suffer the same trauma. The idea was good, but I didn't meet any English man (growing up in a tiny village in the middle of the Loire Valley didn't help either), but I married a French man whose dream was to work abroad.

His job sent us to Argentina, Brazil and China, and we moved to Malaysia after he decided to be his own boss. Argentina was a shock, not because it was a bad country, but because I had so much to learn to adjust to there. Brazil was challenging too, but less so, thanks to what I had learned before. I won't say China was a walk in the park, but it wasn't as challenging as it should have been, even if Mandarin is a totally different ball game when it comes to language learning! My student trauma caught up with me when we arrived in Malaysia as the lingua franca where we live is English. I stressed out for a while, but I told myself, "If you could order a custom-made bedroom in Mandarin and everything arrived the way you wanted it, you can speak English!" And I did!

Along the way, I became a teacher, translator and proofreader in French and English; and both our children are, now, English teachers. It wasn't the journey I had in mind, but I'm happy to have achieved the result I wanted.

Life taught me that in order to thrive, you need to keep an open mind and adjust to circumstances. I would not be where I am now if I had refused to move abroad because I wasn't speaking any foreign languages. It wasn't easy, and I cried more than once, but I kept learning and trying my best. As a result, I'm now fluent in English, Spanish and Portuguese and able to survive in Malay and Mandarin... not bad for someone who's not to supposed to speak anything other than French, right?

Never let anyone (not even you!) tell you what you can't do: you are better than you think!

Valerie Navarro, mum of two young adults, is a bilingual translator and proofreader. She was born in France and lived there for twenty-eight years before following her husband's job around the world with two toddlers in tow. She's now living in a beautiful tropical island in Malaysia with her husband and the kids' cat.

Manners Maketh the Man

Karen Legge

As distant in origin as this proverb, there was a time when my responsibilities were other than packed lunches, folding washing and potty training. There was a time when I had a career and the responsibility of 240 little minds in my lap. There was a time when rapid school improvement was my biggest challenge, not how to get a pre-schooler into clothes and out the door.

Prior to pregnancy, I'd taken on my most demanding role to date; Head of School in a primary deemed to be in 'special measures' by the inspectorate. Imagine the scene: late thirties, newly married, highest of heels, most fitted of dresses. I power-dressed my way in there and was keen to make my mark, but where to start?

You'd be forgiven for thinking the classroom. But with sleeves rolled up, standing at the kitchen servery at lunchtime, I unearthed an issue far greater than a lack of literacy skills or basic numeracy. Manners.

From my earliest memory, the importance of a 'please' or 'thank you' had been rigorously drilled into me. From a 'please may I have…' to a card expressing my delight at a gift, gratitude was ingrained in me.

Respect for my elders was a given. I was always expected to make an effort to talk to adults and not stand mute in the corner. And do you know what, I actually enjoyed it. I loved to be part of the conversation but equally I learned to be a listener too.

So where is the link between a sausage and mash school lunch and the values that were strongly instilled in me as a child?

The grunt.

As I served the snaking line of hungry juniors, I was amazed as they just pointed and grunted at their food of choice!

"Peas or carrots?" I questioned in shock.

"That one," with a stubby pointed finger.

Not a 'peas please' was audible.

Shockwaves reverberated as again and again I had to stress, "Use your words… where are your manners?"

Someone had taken time to prepare their food. Someone had ensured they had a nutritional, warm meal. It wasn't a personal affront that left me reeling, it was a basic display of recognition missing. An appreciation that something had been provided for them. Quite simply: gratitude.

There began my first campaign for change; working with parents on a #greatmanners crusade.

To many it may seem I'd not got my priorities right but

take a moment to think about when someone has shown you manners, when you've felt the warm glow of being valued.

In an age where resources are throwaway, and the pace of life is fast, it's easy to just go about your day without pause. For my son, I desperately want for him to experience gratitude for all he has, build empathy in his relationships and show respect to others. Old-school manners, to me, are the foundation for this and something I will continue to reinforce at every opportunity. Three simple words is all it takes: 'Please' and 'Thank you!'

Karen is an 'unyoung' mum of one; her son being the best fortieth birthday present she could have asked for. Waving goodbye to a twenty-year career in education, she is now a stay-at-home mum in Essex, UK, and thrives on having all sorts of crafty and chaotic adventures with her nearly-four-year-old.

From a Challenging Journey Comes the Greatest Rewards

Joanna Pellereau

In Autumn 2016, we were told the devastating words: 'You are not able to have children without IVF.' When I first considered how to write this story, I wrote a detailed account of our fertility journey. The data, facts, dates, drug names and statistics. The dietary supplements, blood tests, the constant internet searches.

Infertility is something one in six prospective parents has to deal with, and it is not just the inability to have the longed-for baby, it's the potential loss of all your plans for your life. Family gatherings, children's parties, maternity leave, grandchildren(!). It has the potential to 'reset' all your plans and expectations for your life. An infertility diagnosis shatters your heart and sets the path for the coming months and years. The worst thing is feeling alone, like no one understands. You feel that even other people who have been on the journey can't possibly comprehend the depth of your pain and despair. Everyone's emotions are unique.

We chose to take the IVF risk, beginning on Christmas Day 2016. Every day of injections was a feeling of hope, and a feeling of despair that this was necessary. Leaving during friends' wedding speeches to inject hormones; spending every spare moment googling statistics; feeling grateful for the chance and so terribly afraid it wouldn't work. The desperation for the blood tests to come back favourable, for enough eggs, for a good fertilisation rate. The five days of phone calls to hear if those precious four embryos are still going strong. Fear, anger, hope, joy, panic, sadness.

Then the transfer of those precious 200 cells. Optimism, excitement, joy, hope, and fear… Praying that those cells have implanted, that they have divided, that they are growing. Two weeks of waiting to see if there are two lines. OVERWHELMING JOY when they are present. Hugging your mum, meeting her off the train with tears of hope and thankfulness. Texting your best friend and her running round to see the lines. Bad signal meaning family can't hear what you are saying but their excitement when they finally comprehend. Because they have been on this journey with you. You cannot do it alone.

And when I finally held my wonderful son in my arms, and then my precious miracle daughter two years after that, I was so deeply thankful. Thankful for science. Thankful for the embryologists, doctors, midwives and nurses. Thankful for the NHS.

But what about those feelings of upset, inadequacy and loneliness? They are still there. It's still hard to accept we had to follow this path. Every 'accidental' pregnancy is a stab, every 'I wish I wasn't pregnant' hard to hear. And the inadequacy? Well, this journey brought me the unexpected bonus of being accepted to study for a PhD in the area of women's experiences during IVF.

For my two gorgeous children, and for my two precious frozen embryos who have yet to be given their chance at life? Never give up hope. Never give up acknowledging ALL your feelings and emotions. Accept all of yourself, all of your physical and mental limitations. There are always positives in any journey. Things to learn, things to remember and things to forget. We are a mosaic of our experiences. And you, my wonderful children? You are the very best of mine.

Joanna Pellereau is a physics teacher living in Loughborough, UK. Her and her husband Ben have two amazing children through the miracle of IVF. Joanna is an advocate for girls in STEM (Science, Technology, Engineering and Mathematics), a runner, a musician, an avid reader and board game enthusiast, a fan of sci-fi (especially Star Trek) and currently studying for a PhD in education focusing on the experiences of women teachers undergoing fertility treatments.

The Other Side of Heartache Is Strength

Tanya Lynn

After a day spent in the hospital after an ambulance ride and a scare, I didn't want to go home that night because I knew exactly what the conversation was going to be. My relationship ended that night, with what at the time seemed like almost no warning, and I was suddenly six months pregnant and soon to become a single mum. It wasn't the situation or the family I had planned and there was certainly a time when I honestly thought 'I can't do this'. All those plans that we had spent the last few weeks discussing were all gone. I was a young mum and was really not sure of the next steps.

I am incredibly lucky that I had an amazing family support network that kept me going through the motions, made sure I made it to my appointments, made sure I had everything I needed ready. The day arrived and after what luckily was a pretty easy labour compared to many, my beautiful baby girl was born. Within hours of that special moment something in me just clicked and I was so in love with my little bundle of joy. I won't lie, those first few months weren't easy, there were many sleepless nights, but love outweighed those moments. I finally felt like I could do it, I could be the best mum I could be. There were the bad days, but I'm sure we all have them, whether as a mum or not.

A few months later, a man arrived at my door with a court order. Her dad wanted access, and although we are in a good co-parenting place now, we had a few years where we weren't. There were many things we just didn't agree on and struggled to communicate that. It wasn't an easy time and there were a lot of tears, arguments and moments of just such uncertainty. There were days during those times where I felt like a failure and that I did something wrong, and maybe I wasn't good enough. Again, people rallied around, supported me, even my own little girl showed me so much love that I felt things getting better.

Throughout the tears, days of just not having a clue what was going to happen next and if I'd be able to cope with any of it, I know now one thing for sure: I am a much stronger person now because of it. I guess now when bad things happen, and they still do, even at the time when I'm struggling with what's going on, I know I am going to come out the other side, a better person, a stronger person, and someone who can learn from it.

And to my beautiful daughter who is the root of so much of that strength, when bad things happen in your life just know I am going to be by your side supporting you in whatever way I can, and you will come through the other side stronger than you can ever imagine.

Tanya Lynn lives in a market town in the heart of Norfolk, UK. Single mum to her eight-year-old daughter, a social media influencer, she is passionate about saving money and a big fan of musical theatre.

If at First You Don't Succeed, Try, Try Again!

Jane Pesticcio

As I gaze upon my miracle of creation,
I feel such love, pride and celebration!
I realise my baby is part of the circle of life,
Throughout which they will endure pure happiness and strife.

I want you to know how unique and special you are,
Full of talents, qualities; a shining star.
I pray you will use the love and guidance I give,
To be positive and kind around those you live.

My child, life will not always go your way.
You must learn from mistakes and hear what people say.
Please, try to do good and respect others,
Then you will find friendship in your sisters and brothers.

LET ME TELL YOU A STORY…

The more effort you put in and the more you try,
Confidence won't be in short supply!
At first, everything is difficult because it's all new.
All experiences help in the making of you.

It was the same when I wrote poems for my local folk group,
I'd write by hand to keep in the loop.
I'd sit down and read once a month on the stage,
Soon, people loved my work and would readily engage.

Eventually, I wrote enough poems to go in my book,
I sent off my manuscript for the publisher to take a look.
I felt so disappointed as I was kicked to the kerb.
"You are good, but it's not what we want," it said in the blurb.

Not defeated, I still kept on going,
My stories like poems, I kept on sowing.
Then, the pandemic hit and our group went online,
I wrote once a week for most of the time.

My poems told of my daily plight,
How I kept cheerful with hope in sight.
My audience grew and before I knew it a year had passed.
A thoughtful member said to write a book,
"The memories of 2020 will last".

I didn't even have a computer, I know it sounds sad,
If technology goes wrong it drives me mad!
My daughter advised me and a patient publisher too.
Remember, there are people to help, if you're in a stew.

After a lot of hard work, my book was created.
I never thought I would achieve this. I was elated!
You see, you must ALWAYS FOLLOW YOUR DREAMS!
Just keep trying, don't fall apart at the seams.

One day, when the time is right,
If it's meant to be, your hopes will take flight.
It's difficult times that help us to learn,
Only then will we achieve what we yearn.

Remember, life is a journey, a continuous road.
I am always here for you if you wish to offload.
One day, I pray you will become a parent too.
The joy of life bestowed upon you!

Jane Pesticcio is a fifty-six year old mother to four grown-up children, two step children, and five grandchildren! Jane's life is never dull! Originally from Uxbridge, Middlesex, Jane now lives with her husband and stepson (14) in Cardiff, South Wales. Jane loves cycling, swimming and looking after her grandchildren. She's recently published her first book – The Year of 2020 – With Poems Aplenty!

Self-Care Is Essential to Be the Best Version of Yourself!

Charlotte Woods

My passion for self-care and well-being has been born from feeling lost and broken at times. Life is a struggle but only we can help ourselves to ensure we make it the best we can.

Becoming a mum to my wonderful son, Ethan, was a dream come true, but it hasn't come without its stresses and strains. I found it hard to go from being a very independent woman to being so consumed by the love and thinking about my son. Not being able to just pop to the shops or meet friends, everything had to be planned in advance and I had to make sure I didn't leave the house without everything but the kitchen sink! Working for a family business meant that, although I had the best maternity leave having met the most incredible groups of friends in my NCT pregnancy support group, I also couldn't forget work, so balancing everything became something I had to be good at, using every spare moment to work.

Looking back now, those first few years of being a new mum and working were like a whirlwind. My memories of those days are hazy but I remember arriving at our weekly mother and baby class in tears because Ethan hadn't slept well. A thoughtful hug from one of the NCT girls made it all seem better, however within the next few hours we were in the throes of singing, dress-up and flashing lights, this fun-filled world was mixed in with answering work emails about the latest marketing strategy I had created for our suppliers ensuring that we received support to help maintain our marketing budget for the year. This is just a snippet in the day of a life of a working mum.

I felt I was heading for burnout when Covid hit and, although I have not been furloughed over the past year, the time has made me slow down and concentrate on myself more than ever before. If we are not the best version of ourselves then we cannot be there fully for the ones we love. I have now realised that I can't work every evening and every free minute I have, I need to do things for me, I need to be strong and put myself first. If I am not happy and in the right place, then I am no good for my son or partner. This is all new to me, putting myself first, but I am making the most of it and am proud to be included in this book as a step in the right direction.

Self-care can be anything that works for you, mindfulness, exercise, eating healthy, meditation, journaling, coaching, daily affirmations, a daily walk in nature, anything which brings you back to the present and makes you feel content and more fulfilled.

To my beloved son Ethan, it is so important to put yourself first and even more important to show your emotions and to speak about them. Always be honest with how you feel and ask for help. Never suffer alone, always speak to your loved ones and always spend time on self-care so you can be the best version of yourself!

Charlotte Woods is a mum to one very strong-willed three-year-old called Ethan. She lives in Cambridgeshire with her partner Adam and her son. Charlotte is a Marketing Director for her family business but has a deep passion for organising and loves to get involved with any party being planned. You can read about her latest event planning on StyleYourEvent.uk.com. She also has huge passion for self-care and well-being, she has recently set up 'A Day of Calm' to help others feeling the pressure of life, giving people the skills to help them be the best version of themselves.

Put on Your Brave and Be Your Authentic Self!

Sarah Cretegny

It was the last day of the Easter term and I was excited to read in the online school newsletter that you had won the Headmaster's Award. Before I collected you that afternoon, I read the details of what you had been rewarded for doing. It said: 'for working so diligently this term and for always being the first to volunteer to help and support others.'

I could imagine you doing just that, as over the lockdown you had grown in sensitivity and willingness to put the needs of your brother and sister before your own, at least sometimes! I hoped that you could be brave enough to show this side of yourself to your classmates since you'd been back in the classroom.

I was so excited to see what you would say when I picked you up from school an hour or so later. I tried to ask open-ended questions to you and your brother and sister in turn, in the hope to find out something meaningful about your day. We made it all the way home and still no mention of the award. Then we reached the front door and it was then it came out, as you said in a kind of relaxed, timid voice, "Ah yes, I won the Headmaster's Award today," then continuing sheepishly, "I wasn't expecting it. I was just being myself."

It was the last few words that were the gold to me and brought a warm feeling to my heart! Almost without realising, you were being brave to be your true self, showing up in the world authentically, showing people this beautiful part of the true you.

It has taken me decades to be free to show up in this world as my authentic self, and if I'm honest there are still occasions when it's too hard and it takes everything in me to put on my brave and be me. There are the times when the pressure to fit in overwhelms my small voice to speak up for what is right; when I am more concerned about being accepted and not showing my true sensitivity to situations; and when I remain quiet when I'm unsure of my contribution. To hear you say you were just being yourself… that made my heart sing.

Seeing you be brave helps me to be too. The times when I step out in faith for others, offer to pray for them, maybe take a detour to pop in on someone and then not worry that they may think I'm crazy. It's when I take courage and use my sensitivity to encourage others as I share about the things I have overcome.

I'm so proud of you for having the courage to be your true authentic self, at the age of eight years old. I am prouder of you for that than getting any Headmaster's Award!

Being authentic today takes bravery. I know you are brave. I see you being brave, and I long for you to continue being brave and to keep showing up in the world as the whole of you. I believe the world needs to see the whole of you, the whole of me, yes, our natural imperfect selves, the great blend of talents, gifts, strengths and weaknesses that we are. Only when we are our true self, wildly authentic, can the relentless unconditional love of our maker be truly felt and the world is a bit better as a result.

Sarah Cretegny is an English mum of three precious children, Alyssa (10), Talia (8) and Nathan (6). Together with her Swiss husband Raphael, they love life and having been touched by Gods' grace they live life to the full. Connection, creativity and hope are at the heart of everything Sarah does. She started a handmade jewellery business Look Up Jewellery for women who believe beauty starts within. They currently live in Cookham in Berkshire, UK, where you will likely find them messing about on the River Thames as a family or enjoying a few bottles of wine with friends new and old. Home is Lausanne in Switzerland where they love hanging out on the family farm, skiing and eating far too much cheese!

It's All Within You

Laura Cruise

What would you do if you were standing on the edge of a cliff and you weren't sure whether to jump? Now reader, don't worry, I wasn't actually on a cliff, I just felt like I was. People jump off metaphorical cliffs all the time, but perhaps they don't share their story.

My life has had two distinct parts. Part One of my life was a rollercoaster of fun, of excitement, of adventure, of new beginnings. It was a life often full of drama, of tears, of anger and uncertainty. It took me all over the world, pushed me out of my comfort zone, provided me with so many opportunities, gave me three beautiful children and made me happy in many ways – until it didn't anymore. Part One was a life of extremes – amazing highs and then such low lows. After a while the lows overtook the highs and so I found myself standing on the cliff edge.

For many years I wrestled with the big question: if I jumped would I regret it, if I stayed would I regret it?

The answer seemed out of my reach. It was impossible to answer. I can't remember what it was that prompted the urgent need for change but suddenly it was right there in front of me, the decision of my life, and I needed to take action.

I closed my eyes, I held three small sets of hands in mine and together we took a leap into a world we did not know, we did not understand, and for which, I am sure, we weren't really ready for. I jumped with my three babies in the hope that the life that we were going towards was better, was happier, was calmer, was kinder and was much more 'us' than what we had left behind.

Eight years on, I am so grateful that the less confident version of me found it in her to take such a brave move. The life we have created in the subsequent years is even better than I would have ever allowed myself to believe. My Part Two.

It wasn't always easy, and although I questioned my decision at times, I never once regretted it. It was the right choice.

In Part Two I put myself first, challenged myself, took two formal qualifications, bought my own house, proposed to my boyfriend, set my own business up, got married. Became the woman and mum I had always wanted to be. Became confident. Became comfortable in my own skin. Became really happy. Became me!

In Part Two I allow myself to dream and to actually believe I can achieve the things I dream of.

In Part Two I showed my children that life is yours for

the taking, yours for the owning, yours for the dreaming. Your dreams are as valid now as they were when you were small.

No matter what part of your life you are in, hear this: Be a dreamer. Believe in yourself. Believe in your dreams. Don't settle. Work hard, play hard, dream hard and feel the magic when it all comes true. You can make it happen. It's all within you.

Laura runs Laura Cruise Coaching, a business focused on supporting women in Part Two of their lives to identify their dreams and then build the confidence and self-belief to achieve them. A mum and stepmum, she juggles a busy family life alongside her client work, group programmes and communities. Laura believes that we can all achieve our dreams by following her bespoke DREAM method and by truly believing in ourselves.

Count Your Blessings Instead of Sheep

Rose Sayegh

It was one of those nights, where you feel exhausted after a very long day of non-stop running around making sure everyone is healthy, fed, clean and, basically, still alive. I was turning in bed trying all the tricks in the book to fall asleep when I remembered a song I once heard that talks about counting blessings to help you go to sleep, so I thought to myself, why not give it a shot.

It was difficult to decide where to begin. Looking back at my childhood, I can't stop being amazed by how blessed I am for having such amazing parents. My admiration for them grows with every step of my parenting journey. They made it seem so easy.

My second blessing must be my husband. What a blessing of a man he is. How could I have done this without him? He's a combination of a baby's heart, a geek's brain, and an old man's wisdom. The pure definition of a rock. On the other hand, nothing gives me more strength than the strength I get when I stand by his side. He lost the dearest people to his heart in a very short period of time. I was blessed with a lot of strength that I could pass most of it to him to make it through. That makes my strength my third blessing.

Perhaps I should reorder my blessings and move the kids to the top. Oh, those kids. I am forever grateful for having the most amazing stepson anyone could wish for. Without him, I would have been a lousy mother to my own daughters. He taught me how to care and love unconditionally.

I will never forget the emotions I felt in the delivery room when the doctor said "it's a girl" with my first daughter. I was overwhelmed with joy when I heard it again when my second daughter was born.

Not a single day passes by without me thanking whatever power, God or angel is looking after me, helping me look after those three little angels.

My eyes start to close, and I lose count. I'm grateful for our good health, our families and our friends. I'm grateful for my patience. I'm grateful for being faithful to everyone I know. Sometimes I feel grateful just for being grateful because I feel that this is what keeps the blessings coming my way. The list goes on, but I fall asleep before I finish.

I passed this trick to my four-year-old daughter. It doesn't really put her to sleep, as it leads to many discussions and bedtime becomes longer than I would like it to be, but it makes her think of all the things that make her happy. This puts a smile on my face and helps me sleep without having to count blessings or sheep.

Rose Sayegh is a mom of two gorgeous little girls and bonus handsome stepson. She lived in a couple of different places and ended up making a family in the beautiful island of Cyprus. Her hobbies include drinking wine and she is known to give good advice – after her second glass.

Reflect, Get Up and Move On

Amanda Davies

As long as I can remember, I have always been tough, mentally as well as physically. I very rarely got upset, but when I did, my strength truly kicked in. Growing up living next door to her, I would say that my gran was my biggest influence. She was a very proud lady, always dressed immaculately, make up and nails done EVERY day, but was also very friendly and chatty… loved a good old gossip. She reminded me of the mothers in Italian Mafia films, the real head of the families. She was the glue that held us all together really. Family was everything to her.

My gran suffered from both rheumatoid and osteoarthritis. I witnessed her terrible pain, from lying on the sofa to just about being able to walk. But all I can think of when I think of these times was her pure stubbornness, grit and determination. The way of life around me was very much, you have your 'cry', pick yourself up and dust yourself down, and move on. After all, living in the past serves no purpose at all, only as a lesson learnt. This is something that would serve me in a way that I could never have imagined in years to come.

When I married my husband and we decided on starting a family, I didn't think I would have any problems conceiving. I was very wrong. Sadly, we would need IVF, and the journey that we were about to embark on would really test my belief system that had been built up over the best part of thirty years, and have me question it in a big way. I would need ten rounds of IVF to be able to have my beautiful baby girl (who is actually five!). At the start, my gran was always there to encourage me not to give up and say that it would happen, with that stubbornness that she had. I truly believe that without this frame of mind, I would have given up after the first round. But for me, giving up was not in my vocabulary, and my stubbornness kicked in.

This strength would be called upon even more two years after my daughter was born, when I lost my baby. Conceived again through IVF, I lost it just short of twelve weeks and then went on to have a major haemorrhage and nearly lost my life. I lost all confidence and trust in my strength and my belief system. I ended up with PTSD, panic and anxiety attacks. I really lost my way for the best part of three years, and that's okay, but those beliefs and words kicked back in and helped me fight my way back to who I was before all the 'terrible' happened, albeit a little wiser.

Life is tough. There is no getting away from the fact

that there will be ups and downs, joyous and heartbreaking times. It's how we are taught and subsequently deal with the tough times that will truly define us. Well, this is my view anyway.

No matter what life throws at you, know that you have an inner strength that will help you cope and survive.

Amanda is a forty-something mother of one. She lives in South Wales with her husband, their five-year-old daughter and dog. She is a Sports Massage Therapist and Holistic Therapist, and a Business Manager for a new dance school. Amanda enjoys creating activities for her daughter and family time. She loves walking and discovering new places and enjoys learning. She is also a craft enthusiast.

You're Wonderful the Way You Are

Patrice Payment

If I could jump in a time machine and go back to 1996, the year I started high school, there are many things I'd tell my fifteen-year-old self about life. I'd start by telling myself to stop worrying so much about what other people think. This is one thing that I want most for my kids to learn from me.

I probably spent the first thirty-something years of my life trying to be someone else so that people would like me. If only I knew then what I know now. I imagine I wouldn't have made so many mistakes and I probably would have enjoyed the first half of my life more. I wouldn't have just gone along with what everyone else was doing because I didn't want to say no.

Looking back, I can see how much time I spent fighting

so hard to please everyone else but myself. It's easy to do. During my teens and twenties, I was so focused on what other people would think if I was myself. I tried to hide what my beliefs and values were. I was constantly holding back and afraid to speak up when I saw people doing things I didn't agree with. I was always so shy and just kept most of my thoughts to myself.

Now that I'm approaching forty this year, I'm starting to realize that I can't waste any more time being someone that I'm not. It's really liberating to just be myself and not who everyone else wants me to be. Now if I'm thinking something I say it. And when someone says something I don't agree with, I tell them.

I wish my kids could see how important it is to be yourself sooner than I did. I want them to know that there is no point in wasting so much time being someone else. The people that don't like you for who you really are aren't worth your time.

When it comes the time to find your partner in life, it's even more important to be who you really are. The person you spend the rest of your life with is going to learn more about you than you ever could have imagined. They're going to learn who you really are eventually, so why waste your energy trying to impress them being someone else? I know this may be something that you just have to learn through experience. But I hope that I can save you from more heartache than necessary.

So just be yourself. Let that pressure to be perfect go because you don't need to be anyone else. Don't ever stop dancing to the music in the kitchen, even if it means you're dancing to the beat of a different drum. You are wonderful just the way you are.

Patrice Payment lives in Atlanta, Georgia, where she blogs about the challenges of being a mom on Mom Life With P. Patrice is a former child therapist whose passion is helping others, especially moms that struggle with anxiety and depression. On the weekends you'll find her spending time outdoors hiking, running, or watching her boys play sports.

Ultimately, We're a Product of Our Decisions, Not Our Circumstances

Ndah Mbawa

My darlings, never forget that you are enough. Always are. Always will be. And as much as is in your power and knowledge, make decisions consciously. Indecision is also a decision, so when you are undecided, let it be by choice sweet pea. Here's a little story. Maybe, it'll help you understand your mum's strengths and flaws.

For a forty-three-year veteran of motherlessness (at the time of writing), it's bizarre that until seven years ago, I felt like an imposter trying to own that truth. It came home to roost when Grandpa passed on seven years ago. You'd think I would be constipated with facts and experiences of what it means for me, a girl child, to wear this sad badge of having no mum… it's hardly so.

Grandpa did his best to fill the void of motherlessness. So, in his last days, it became obvious that I would be orphaned in a day. Hence, most Mother's Days, I weep bitterly for he was also my mother, a fantastic one too. One who taught me to be kind, courageous and have little regard for ceilings. I'd also weep for my younger self who grew up without a mum's gatekeeping or lighthouse presence; for losing what I didn't know I had. I'd weep for the scars of a childhood featuring a stepmother I felt had no ability or willingness to nurture those who weren't hers. One whose legacy once included my burning desire to be a better person than she ever was… cue people pleasing. I also weep for you and your grandparents, who missed the chance to spend time together.

Having Kaitlyn the same year we lost Grandpa was an epiphany. I saw motherhood differently through grief-tinted glasses. Life was taken and given. I decided to let the film of depression lift. It'd been humming away inaudibly since we lost your sister Mischa in 2006, giving momentum to my insecurities. Mothering is part instinct, part training and part personality, but when one is motherless so young, instinct and personality may struggle to make up for lack of training. That was my story.

Soon, I realised that in taking "too much mothering advice/inspiration" because of a lack of confidence in my ability or qualification to adequately mother, I was still making a decision, albeit unconsciously. A decision not to mother according to my outlook, values, unique experiences and, more grievously, a decision not to mother according to your unique needs and personalities.

Consequently, I decided that God was no fool to gift me with three bright and beautiful girls to call my own. I decided to continue doing my best, knowing that I was exactly the mother you needed, were destined to have or chose to have. I decided not to let childhood circumstances or inadequacies determine the future or be a joy suck of the present. I decided to be thankful that, in spite of my insecurities, I showed up every day as best as I could because of my boundless love for you. I decided to be okay with being a work in progress as a mum. I decided to be grateful for the times you test or take me for granted the most; it shows the confidence you have in my love.

So, darlings, choose your decisions wisely and consciously.

Ndah Mbawa lives in Northampton with her husband and three daughters (Kirsten (13), Aiyven (12) and Kaitlyn (6)). A freelance IT Business Analyst by day and a writer by calling, she runs Etinde House Company, an artisan outfit producing chilli oils, chilli pastes, snacks and spice rubs. Ndah also helps run Mbawa Books, a small publishing house set up for her two older daughters who are published authors and founders of Happier Every Chapter, a book subscription box for eight to fourteen year olds.

Live the Life of Your Dreams

Rosaleen Hird

You don't need anybody's permission to live the life of your dreams. The life that's in your dreams. I didn't get that memo and I based my major life choices on what others thought was right for me, what others approved of. You are very likely to create moments of misery by doing that; dare I say long periods of misery rather than moments. That's not to say you'll avoid misery even when following your soul's desires, the point of this is not to avoid misery or sadness or any less favourable emotions, that's all part of living. The aim is for a life without regrets.

It feels like I spent a lifetime, around thirty years, doing things that would receive approval from others. Some of those people were dear to me, I valued their opinion; others were simply passers-by, literally and figuratively. I was afraid of letting people down, of disappointing them, of having to explain why I didn't follow their advice, of them not loving me; in short, I was afraid of almost everything.

If I had truly listened to my inner voice, I might have chosen a different university degree. I start at that point because it feels like I had the most choice over my life then, the start of adulthood perhaps. I could go back earlier than that. Would I have chosen different subjects to study at sixth-form college, different additional classes to attend, different friends to spend my time, my life, with? I might not have listened to the careers advisor who guided me away from a career as a writer and journalist because "anybody can write". I might have listened to my heart and had courage in the knowledge that I loved writing and reading and that doing something purely for the love of it was the best place to start.

Instead, I did as I was told and chose a more sensible option. And there followed years of doing what was expected of me, of choosing the more sensible option, of not leaving relationships when they were over, instead allowing them to deteriorate like that piece of mouldy cheese at the back of the fridge, where you hope that somebody else will deal with it so you don't have to, but nobody does, resulting in a stinky fridge and that mould tainting other things too. It was a pattern I repeated, until I found myself in a marriage that I didn't want or actively choose. I managed to find myself out of it, but it wasn't quite as easy as the stroll I'd taken into it. Not recommended.

It wasn't until a few months before meeting Daddy that I started making choices based on what I really wanted in life. And then like anything it just became a habit, the more I chose for myself the more I invited what I really wanted into my life, and the more joy I experienced. And then I had you. And that's when I realised that I had changed as a person when I became a mother, despite my resistance to that cliché, and so what I wanted changed too. I began to reconsider how I could live the life of my dreams, a life where my children were the epicentre.

Rosaleen Hird is a mother of two, soon to be mother of three. She's a wife, daughter, sister, a holistic therapist, a Weleda well-being advisor and a discoverer of joy. Rosaleen is based in Yorkshire, in the UK, where there's not quite enough sunshine for her liking but beautiful surroundings.

Look Past What You See on the Surface

Joanne Kendal

The struggles! The days when life is tough, and it is difficult to know what to do next. NO ONE has got their shit together. None of us know what we're doing and most of us never have done. We all started with a plan but then life gets in the way. Social media will have you think that possessions, cosmetic surgery, a well-sculpted body and a plane ticket will solve all of your problems. What you won't see is the pain, the loneliness, the days when things are just too much and the risks those people took and take every day, the worries, the anxiety and the losses. Believe me, in real life, we have them all. That's not to say that life isn't amazing and that you can't achieve spectacular things. I know you will. I also know that the good days are worth every rubbish day, but you will enjoy it tenfold if you're not comparing each step you take with someone else's.

Growing up my self-esteem had always been really low, but I always had big plans of how I would change that. Lose those extra pounds, get that dream job, have that dream relationship, perfect outfits and live somewhere sunny and exciting. If I worked for all that then I'd be happy. So, I did it all. I got a degree, I travelled, I moved away, I had a beautiful wedding, we had a lovely home, lovely cars, but I wasn't completely happy because I was constantly comparing myself to other people. As a mum, the pressure over boils. I wanted the perfect products for you, I wanted to take you to all these great places and to be a "perfect mummy". On top of that I needed to lose the baby weight and work to pay the bills – but not too much because, even though I needed to provide a great life for you, I also felt the pull to be with you simultaneously. It took its toll and I experienced severe postnatal depression. I am still battling this almost nine years later. It has taken a lot of hard work, but I have sought professional help and I can't stress enough how important asking for help is.

The demands from social media, magazines, self-help books, TV, etc. distort the good work I put in every day to feel 'enough'. You will never find the answers for anything in these places. Speak to me and your dad (we will always be here for you), speak to your grandparents, your friends, your work colleagues, whoever is in your life. Get a real picture. Exchange stories about your struggles and laugh about the mistakes you make. You don't need a million opinions from social media or a million edited stories about how someone else is doing. You need the real people in your tribe who have been through it all and know that some days are just rubbish, you won't always feel blessed and life isn't always easy.

I suppose the main thing I want to say to you is that you are enough just as you are, don't ever compare to others because there is no comparison, we are all travelling on our own path and our stories will never start and end the same. Just enjoy the journey.

Joanne is a school admin assistant from Manchester (UK). She is a devoted mummy to Charlie and Willow and enjoys spending time with her husband and their little family, including their fur baby Wilson the sausage dog.

Live for Now, Not the Future

Louisa Douglas

When I was a child, I dreamed of being all the things that most children dream of. As I grew up and was getting closer to needing to select a likely vocation, many of my choices were met with rebuttals.

"That won't earn you enough money."

"That's not a stable career path."

"More people fail at that than succeed."

These advisories were all delivered with love and the best intentions – to help me select a career that would give me stability and earn enough to live comfortably, therefore lead me to a happy and fulfilled adulthood. What none of us realised at the time was the impact of this advice and how it shaped the way I would approach the world. What these cautions really did was teach me to worry about the future and inhibit my enjoyment of the present day.

When I was eighteen, I did a six-month work placement in Canada. It was hands down the most enjoyable experience of my life. Whilst out there I wanted to extend my stay; however, worries about saving money for university brought me home at the end of my planned trip.

Fast forward a couple of years, university hadn't worked out, but I was paving my way in my career when an old friend reached out inviting me to join him in Australia on a working visa. A friend and I were in the process of buying a property, but even she said I would be a fool to pass up this experience for the sake of our flat.

Then the worries started. I worried about not being able to get on the property ladder again in the future. About what I would do for work there as there were limitations on how long you could work for one company. And about what I would then do for work when I inevitably had to come home. I decided not to go.

After a while, I realised that every life decision I made in young adulthood had future-me in mind. I'd lost the ability to do something big just because I wanted to. It stopped me from travelling, it stopped me from taking certain jobs, it has caused a lot of regret for me.

Once I made this realisation, it firmed one positive thing for future-me: I would not let my children live their lives in the same way. Long before children were even on the cards for me, I made this pledge:

> *I will encourage my child to follow their dreams, I will encourage them to travel, if they wish to do so, and enjoy life knowing that the future will sort itself out in the end.*

Someone once said to me it's better to regret the things you did over the things you didn't, and this rings very true for me. If I do make a decision I later regret, I always have solace in the fact that at least I tried. Whereas, for all of those things I didn't do, I still wonder what could have been.

Now you are here my darling H, and soon to join us, little bump, whatever you want to be I'll support you. Whatever you want to do, I'll help you find a way. You'll blaze trails, I just know you will, and I'll be by your side the entire way.

Louisa is mum of one cloth bum little H, with another one on the way. Based in Hampshire, UK, Louisa tries to live a more sustainable lifestyle for her children. She shares her eco swaps and parenting experience on her blog Cloth Bum Mum.

Being Different Can Be a Blessing

Laura Bland

Children are curious, it is in their nature. At a young age, they have no filter between their thoughts and what comes out of their mouth and, quite honestly, I view that as both a blessing and a curse, as I'm sure many other parents do. As we grow older, it is instilled in us that we should think before we speak, that we shouldn't stare and that we shouldn't ask questions, but that loss of open curiosity creates barriers. Barriers that we might not even notice to begin with but nevertheless are there.

When we stop being curious, when we stop asking questions, when we stop engaging in conversations, we lose those connections that could have been. We narrow our own lives, our ability to be understanding and empathetic, and most of all we stop learning.

You see we are all different, different thoughts, different feelings, different backgrounds, different experiences and different looks. That last one is true in our house. We are a pretty average family in many respects, a loving mum and dad to our daughter, who is the centre of our world, but we are also different, and we are different in a way that you can see.

Our 'different' is that my partner is an amputee, he has no right leg from just below his knee, he wears a prosthetic limb, but it clearly looks different. In some ways this has been a blessing in disguise for us. The amputation was carried out when our daughter was just fifteen months old, so for her that missing limb is perfectly normal. She didn't bat an eyelid when I took her for that first hospital visit, all she saw was daddy and not the fact that he was now different.

We have an incredible empathetic, kind and generous daughter, she accepts people fully just for who they are. Differences of any kind do not matter, all she is bothered about is if they are kind and will be a good friend, and this is exactly as it should be. In reception class at school our daughter won an award for being kind and always trying to help others if they are upset or struggling; I hope this is how she will always remain.

When we go out, we get 'the looks', judgement, particularly from older people and especially when we pull into a disabled parking space; they seem to think we should not be there. We also get 'the looks' from children, but they are the looks of curiosity and wonder, they are the looks of intrigue and interest. They are the looks that say, 'tell me more, so I can understand better', they are not the looks of judgement. Those are the looks we welcome, and we will always stop and explain, or give a closer look.

My role as mum is to support and nurture and to raise an honest, kind and accepting daughter. So far, I seem to be winning at that. My wish now is that she always looks with eyes that say 'tell me more, so I can understand better' and not with eyes of judgement.

Laura Bland is a mother of one and is based in Leicestershire, UK, with her daughter and partner and their crazy cat Lilo. She is a writer at heart, and this will be her ninth book to be published. She loves to support other women in any way that she can.

There Is No Practice Life, This One Is All You Have!

Danielle Fraser

Be that person.

The person who is not afraid to be themselves.

One who has guts and is brave enough to follow your dreams.

The person who has the courage to go out and get what you deserve.

Be the person with a voice to stand up for what you believe in.

I once knew a girl who would avoid anything that involved talking in front of an audience, didn't apply for that job because she didn't believe in herself, a girl that turned down so many opportunities and didn't push herself enough because the fear of failure got the better of her.

She spent far too long allowing other people to hold her back, letting her fears hold her back.

She was scared of other people's opinions.

She feared failure but, even more so, she feared success.

She doubted her potential.

But then she became a mother, and over time grew in confidence.

She grew as a person, figured out who she was and what her purpose was.

That she is ME.

It took me years to find my passion.

Years of courses, college, university and still unsure of the path to my future.

It wasn't until a couple of years back from the time of me writing this that I finally found my passion, my vision, my excitement. The career that I was certain was for me for the rest of my life.

Yet it can all be taken away from you in the blink of an eye!

Just planning to launch my business and then came my diagnosis of Functional Neurological Disorder.

Right now, I feel incapable, I feel unwell and uncertain of what lies ahead.

My condition might get better, and I might recover, or it may well progress. Every day is very different, I have no idea how I might feel day to day, minute to minute.

However, I must think. I have so many goals, so many

dreams and so much I want to achieve in life. I want to build a legacy for you – my beautiful children.

You cannot let it hold you back.

The fears, the what ifs.

Maybe I won't get to have the career I was dreaming of, maybe I won't get to launch my dream business now, but it does not mean I cannot be successful doing something else.

I love to journal, to write and recently many opportunities have arisen, doors have opened for various writing projects such as this one. Who knows where this might take me?

I trust that everything is going to be okay, that everything will work out in the end.

Whatever challenges you might face, just keep going, take chances, take risks because life is full of mistakes and experiences, ups and downs, good times and bad.

The struggles will make you stronger.

You can cry and scream and have an off day, but you do not get to quit!

You will find the strength to get back up and one day I know you will fly.

Danni Fraser is thirty-four and lives in Oxfordshire. She is a proud mama to four children, Taya 17, Caitlyn 14,

Leuan 7 and Edie 2. She is a self-love advocate and loves to empower women. She loves to read, write and blog and survives pretty much on caffeine to get her through the day!

My Choices Are Not Your Burden

Denise Cornell

The alarm buzzed at 4:45am. By 5:20 we're on the road.

Covered in the distinctive smell of horse and dust, it's nearly 3pm before we're back home.

She's off to shriek into the phone about her first reserve grand champion while I unload the car, start the laundry and slide into the bathtub for a long soak.

Soon, she's hurriedly knocking on the bathroom door. "Mom! I'm hungry and there's nothing to eat. When's dinner?"

"Okay. I'll be out in a minute," I replied, begrudgingly.

Her brother and I are at the table. Waiting.

"Did she hear you call her for dinner?"

"Yes," he grunted, in that way only teenage boys can do, mustering a generation of disdain in one guttural sound.

We start without her.

Eventually, with her dinner half-eaten, she pushes her plate forward and declares, "I'm done. Can we go? Sarah's waiting."

"Are you kidding me? I thought you were starving? I got out of the tub to make dinner for you and…" I stammered.

Without pause, she looked straight at me and said, "I didn't ask you to get out of the tub. You chose to get out. Don't put that on me."

She was right. Infuriatingly right.

Here I was, again, facing that blurry line between mother and martyr.

I had chosen to put mothering before myself – when it absolutely wasn't necessary. (At age thirteen, she can make herself a snack.) And then I laid my choice squarely at her feet, like my decisions were somehow her responsibility.

She's right. It's not "on her", but that's right where I put it with all the ugly implied guilt: I got out of the tub for you. You should be grateful.

Ouch.

I'm horrified at how naturally this scene unfolded, like it's part of my DNA.

That's the power of generational patterns in motion, perpetuating the lies of sacrifice and guilt.

Now it's back on me, and it would be so easy to double down and drag another generation with me.

But not today. Not on my watch. She will not learn this from me.

So, let me be clear, dear daughter…

You are not responsible for other people's actions. Their choices are not your burden.

As an observer of this story, you may think I've stretched to pull these lessons from one mundane part of our day.

I have not.

I see my children watching and listening.

I see them absorbing the undercurrents of my mothering, like my knee-jerk reaction to ignore my own needs and be resentful about it.

On this day I catch myself.

The Holy Mother of Martyrdom myth stops with me.

So, with wounded pride, I look at her and say, "You're right. You're exactly right. I'll take you to Sarah's as soon as I'm done eating."

As she hurries out of the car she calls back, "Thanks for dinner, Mom. Bye. I love you."

Denise Cornell writes in service to the examined life, to answering the creative call, and her personal philosophy of Truth Over Strategy. She lives in Austin, Texas, with her two children.

Rule the World

Vicky Robinson

There's that popular quote, the one that says how one day the meek will inherit the Earth. I always hoped that this would come true for me, and now for you, my two beautiful children.

Like my mum, I was painfully shy growing up, with what we would describe nowadays as social anxiety. I still struggle, but I have learnt ways to overcome some of the barriers that were holding me back.

Back then, tears would come to my eyes if I had to wait to be picked to join a group or if I had to give a presentation in front of my class. My face would burn hotter than the sun and I would retreat to my place of safety, inside my head. However, little did I know, I was on a path of self-actualisation. I would learn and grow in the way that was right for me, and you, my children, will do the same.

Both of you deal with your shyness in very different ways, one of you completely withdraws and refuses to speak, and the other fights their way out of those uncomfortable feelings. I want you both to know that I understand, as I have been there too. Being a shy person can mean that people judge us negatively, label us as being weird or awkward. However, being a shy and sensitive person is also equated with being an empath, a good listener, being sensitive to the needs of others, and being kind and caring. I can honestly say that you both have these qualities in abundance and make me proud every day.

Lewis, you have taught me how to fight for what I believe in; when your dad and I divorced it was me and you against the world. You had your difficulties throughout school, and I fought to get you what you needed to progress. As I became a mum, my shyness took a back seat because you were my priority.

Amelia, you have taught me how to be brave. Despite the fact that you had a cancerous brain tumour, you had brain surgery and then had Proton Beam Therapy in an entirely different country, you carried on playing like nothing had happened. After nine hours of brain surgery, you woke up and asked if you could go to the playroom. Your left-sided weakness only lasted a couple of days because you were determined to get up and play.

Because of you, my wonderful children, I am a better, stronger person. You are both amazing, unique, caring, kind, generous, loving individuals and I am proud to be your mum. Despite all of our difficulties, we stick together and carry on. Together we can achieve anything, together we can rule the world.

Vicky Robinson is a mother of two, a stepmother of two and an ex-stepmother of one with whom she still has a fantastic relationship. Vicky is also a mum to three rescue cats. Born in Bradford, West Yorkshire, Vicky still resides in the area. Vicky loves to study, has a BSc in Learning Disability Nursing, a foundation degree in early years and is soon to be qualified as a counsellor.

Listen to Your Heart

Polina Volkova

There are so many thoughts fighting in my head about what the most important lesson is I could teach my children. How can you choose when you want to pour all the information into them to avoid them making the same mistakes you made? Unfortunately, we can't just press a magic button and download an antivirus that protects our children from everything. It's our karma to watch them make wrong choices from time to time and remember how we, too, were warned about the same things by our parents, and how it flew in one ear and escaped from the other. We all thought we knew better, before we realised that we really never knew anything at all. Only your own life experience can teach you that.

I guess what I really want them to learn is how to listen to their heart and passion they hold within them, whatever it may be. Funnily enough, that was the first song by Roxette that I sang during my adult singing lesson. I felt so silly going to sing in my thirties, but it felt wonderful. I didn't end up with a platinum-selling album but loved every minute. The truth is we don't have to be amazing at what we love – we just need to love doing it. Too often as adults we forget how to enjoy feeling good just for the sake of it.

My mum always scared me that if I didn't study well, I would end up working at the post office – that was the epitome of an awful life according to her. And I feel that opinion is so flawed. We have so many misconceptions and stereotypes of what a miserable life is. What is "hell on earth" for one person is another person's dream. What if you love to deliver post, work individually and have an active lifestyle? Then working there would be perfect for you. We don't have to be successful and wealthy to be happy. And we can also be miserable while extremely successful. I want my children to do what makes them happy – driver, chef, dancer or entrepreneur.

Happiness is a journey, not a destination and it's okay to change direction and stop from time to time. I'm forty this year and I still haven't worked out what I want to do, but I have progressed to NOT doing what I don't enjoy doing as life is too short for that. What drives me as a person is helping people. It makes me truly happy like a little child that sees a cake or a balloon. When I was in a philosophy class in college in my twenties, the teacher asked us, "Is it a selfish thing to help people when you're doing it only to feel good about yourself?" I still haven't worked out that riddle, but what I do know is society is a better place if people are getting their kicks from helping people.

In fact, I also listened to my heart when we started our little family – we had no security, family back up or stability, but we did have the burning desire to make it work. And here we are, ten years into our marriage, moving between four continents and two kids later, still listening to the whisper in our hearts (when the kids are quiet enough to let us hear it).

Polina Volkova was born in USSR and is a wife to Jose and mother to two Russian Colombian boys, Elmer and Ivan. She was one of the first Russian students in an English boarding school in 1992 where she learned all the ways not to parent. Polina originally studied/worked in marketing and since having kids has developed her luxury brand and become a designer clothes reseller with her "fashion divas" eBay boutique. She is passionate about sustainability, preserving nature, nutrition and parenting. She dreams of rescuing a dog or cat once the other creatures at her home are older and wiser.

Never Give Up, and Stay Strong

Rebecka Jeyes

So, it was back in the beginning of March 2020. I had just become a single mother. I was four months pregnant, and I already had a lively, energetic and loving sixteen-month-old. COVID-19 had just become a thing, although at this stage we had no idea what was ahead of us and was yet to come. Joseph (my eldest) had recently developed a cough as he had a chest infection. Due to guidelines at the time, we were told we had to self-isolate.

I remember sitting on the sofa downstairs. Alone. Joseph was asleep upstairs. I just cried, and the biggest thought that came to my mind was, "How am I going to do this? I can't do this on my own."

It was a scary time with this new virus that we didn't know much about, and the start of my new journey into single motherhood. I was not prepared for this. I had just come out of a bad relationship that left me with low self-esteem. I can honestly say this had been the hardest time in my life. Having to rebuild myself, look after a toddler and grow another human being all at the same time. With the uncertainty of how any of this was going to pan out. It was daunting.

Jacob soon came along, and yes it was difficult at the beginning, but we got through it. I had to develop new routines, I had to carry on with my life and be strong for my children, whilst also fighting my own demons. At the age of eighteen, I was diagnosed with depression, and it is something that I have had to live with every day of my life.

I have not had it easy. Just like many other people, I have faced many challenges. There have been times where I have wanted to give up. One thing you must always remember is that it is never as bad as it seems at the time, and things will get better. You are always going to have problems to face, you are always going to have difficult times. You have to take the good with the bad. Just remember that it too will pass.

I have more bad days than good days. Nevertheless, I am strong like my mum. I know I won't give up because since having you two amazing boys, my life has purpose. You are the reason I wake up in the morning, and you are the reason why I keep fighting.

To my children. I want you to know, you saved my life. It is you that keeps me going, it is you that I live for. When everything feels wrong, when things are tough, it is you my dear boys that help me to carry on. I don't have time to sit and wallow. I have to be there for you. Don't ever give up and make rash decisions on a bad day because I guarantee you it will always look better in the morning.

You're stronger than you think you are, never give up.

Rebecka is twenty-five years of age. She is a single mother to two handsome and amazing little boys. Originally from England, but now residing in Northern Ireland, Rebecka works as a Nursery Assistant. Rebecka is just your average mum, who sometimes does not get everything right, and she is not afraid to admit motherhood is the hardest but most rewarding thing she has ever had to do.

Dream Big, Don't Limit Your Potential

Laura Edgson

When I was young, I used to love listening to Nanny Mary tell me stories about her young life in London post war, what she was like as a child. Weaved in among the stories of skipping school in the 1950s and 60s to spend the day riding horses, swimming, or hiding in the library, was the story of a young woman who felt inadequate, who felt that she lacked the capability to learn, and so she squashed her dreams and settled. Later in life, she pursued those dreams (maybe it is something that comes with age and life experience); she taught herself to spell by studying the dictionary, to play chess from a book (I've still never beaten her!) and has dedicated her life to acquiring knowledge and skills because that's what she loves. Maybe not grand plans for some, but it was her dream, and she realised it with sheer stubbornness and determination, something you have inherited.

I was always scared of expecting too much, spent much of my younger life settling for second best – with relationships, jobs, life – because it was all I believed I was capable of. I was wrong. My only limit was my own self-belief, which I am constantly working on. Somewhere in my late twenties something finally clicked, and I learned that I needed to find out what I was for. I spent eleven years by myself, trying to find out who I was, what I stood for, and what I could do, and I finally realised that I deserved better. I just wish it hadn't taken me thirty-something years to discover it.

I don't want that for you. I want you to realise your worth and potential, to take your dreams and soar because I see the passion and drive in you to follow your dreams. But I also see your uncertainty and self-doubt sometimes. You may say I'm biased, that every mother sees the same in their child. Doesn't make it any less true; doesn't make you any less capable.

Your Auntie Emily (you were too young when she died to really remember her) faced a debilitating disease and the ever-present shadow of the grim reaper with such a zest for life, for squeezing every drop of joy out of the day. She packed more into the few years I knew her than most people do in a lifetime. She left a lasting imprint on me; a legacy of seizing every opportunity because you just don't know when you may get another chance. She was my hero.

And, as you know, your Auntie Jayne is a perfect role

model for always having plans (usually multiple at once!) and making them happen. Never one to shy away from dreaming, and then putting in the hard work to make it reality, she is the epitome of ambition, of dreaming big.

So, whether you choose to be a 'police-y' or a fashion designer, a palaeontologist or security guard, always believe in your potential and know that I will support you. I am immensely proud of you. It won't always be an easy path, but with dedication and passion, getting there will be so much more satisfying. Listen to your heart and do what makes you happy. Don't be afraid to dream big.

Laura Edgson is mother to two adult humans and a fur baby. She lives in South Wales and runs a Greek restaurant with her partner, alongside studying for an English Literature degree, learning Greek, and cleaning up the never-ending mess made by aforementioned children! She loves books, long walks and lots of coffee.

Healing Yourself: The Ultimate Super Power

Liz Clifton

S*mash!*

I threw the cup into the sink.

Worried by the ear-splitting crack, I crept over and gazed through a three-inch hole down to the cupboard below.

Barely making it through another day; Avy baby was washed, dressed, fed and having a nap.

Still in my dressing gown, I was just about to wash up and start preparing food for when Sti got back from school.

Now I couldn't. I screamed and ran upstairs into our tiny bathroom.

Crumpling to the floor, I curled up tight in the corner by the toilet, sobbing uncontrollably.

At that moment, I felt completely overwhelmed, alone and hopeless.

Heart racing, head fizzing, I sank down, feeling faint.

Something had to change.

My first step was looking into anger, stress and how to find balance.

It's been a loooooong journey for me.

Years later in leadership training, I remembered that hole in the sink.

My own wounds rushed through me, connecting my emotional support gaps with the broken sink.

Crashing fiercely as stormy waves swept fast revealing themselves to me.

Again, I sank to the floor and sobbed with every cell in my body and every part of my being.

The stabbing pain of cruel words from bullies cut deep, internal struggle with eating disorders, dullness of postnatal depression, volunteering to become the weekend parent after divorce, abuse, miscarriage and supporting a close family member through addiction, I could finally see myself in all my bedraggled glory.

No matter what my journey had been so far, I was here, healthy, full of love, curiosity and drive to start finally healing myself.

Having supported so many others by putting them first throughout my life, I finally began to look after myself too.

This was a huge learning curve, which I resisted completely at first.

How on earth could spending time on me be the answer when I felt that I was already letting everyone else down?

Through excavating my deep-rooted self-limiting

belief that I wasn't good enough, I was gradually able to heal myself.

Realising that you are able to love deeper when you allow yourself to receive love first is priceless.

Having always seen myself as caring and supportive, it stung to grasp that not allowing others to love and support me meant that I was holding back some of my love from them.

My belief is that love is a healing super power cycle, which we can receive and give in an ever-flowing unison.

The more we allow ourselves to be loved, healed and cared for, the more we are able to give to others.

It's an ongoing process as new repressed emotions continue to pop up and life keeps presenting new opportunities.

Today those feelings of overwhelm are gone.

With a clear vision for my life, I have direction, skills, tools, beliefs and a map to get me there and support you on your journey too.

Feeling alone is in the past since I discovered my voice and the confidence to get support when I need it. Use your beautiful voice to keep spreading love in the world.

My hopelessness has disappeared, replaced by excitement, love, light and gratitude as I wake each morning for the gift of that day.

Thank you, thank you, thank you, for the love light that you shine in our lives. Love you so much, girls xxxx

Liz Clifton is a mum of four gorgeous girls, two Romanian rescue dogs and a wife living in Caerphilly, Wales, UK. She loves reading, writing, cooking, gardening, dancing, craft, walking, singing, having fun and giggling with family. She is a Reiki Master, NLP Practitioner, Love Light Leader and Coach supporting others to heal, evolve and thrive.

Accept Your "Self"

Asta Mail

To the children of this new world:

I give you my gratitude and respect simply for being here and reading this. Your focus and time are your most valued attributes in life, and I am honored that you can give some of them to my words in this moment.

> *To be beautiful means to be yourself.*
> *You don't need to be accepted by others.*
> *You need to accept yourself.*
>
> Thich Nhat Hanh

So, my child, who are you?

This is a question you will face throughout your life. Believe it or not, you are a collection of cells that have spontaneously diversified to become a living, breathing, functional meat machine.

But that's not all you are, is it? You know full well that

there is so much more to you than that.

So, who are you? Don't be surprised or dismayed if this answer changes day to day.

We all have an idea of what we want to be, and sometimes we have a better idea of who we don't want to be. Knowing these things does not necessarily imply that you know who you truly are.

I invite you to consider that the most valuable thing you can do with your time and your focus is to gain a better understanding of yourself. The journey to self-understanding is a long and ever-unfolding path, but it is one of the most impactful experiences you will have while you're inhabiting this meat suit of yours.

You can begin by exploring what you like and dislike. What moves you to tears of sadness, or tears of joy? What makes your pulse quicken, and your body coil like a spring to propel you into action? How does joy, sadness, anger, frustration and serenity feel to you?

There is a whole world waiting to be explored inside your mind. I find that one of the best ways to explore who you are is by exploring the world while you're at it.

When you are in motion, travelling through the world, you are freed by the expectations that others have of "who you are". You are free to evolve your sense of self, and you expose yourself to situations and experiences you may never have at home.

In each moment, you choose the way you create and respond to the world. Your actions, and your reflection on those actions, allow you to better realize what you stand for, what your moral compass tells you, and what leads you towards a life that feels well lived.

Don't be surprised if there are parts of yourself that you discover and don't like. We are all both good and bad, kind and mean, righteous and self-sabotaging. It is in our nature to be dualistic. If you can meet these parts of yourself with acceptance and grace, you can integrate them, understand them, and even sometimes release them as you grow into a person more in tune with who you want to be.

When you can find understanding in yourself, it is so much easier to find understanding in others.

So go, beautiful children. Travel, explore, be curious. Look out at the wonder of nature and look in at the nature of your miraculous being.

You are loved. You are safe, secure, protected and connected. You are alive!

Asta Mail is a mom first, and an adventurer second! She works as an education coordinator for a conservation foundation in Victoria, British Columbia, Canada. Asta splits her time between the Zoom screen and the deck of a teaching sailboat, where she brings students out on the water to experience the magic of Mother Nature. Asta, her husband Andrew and her daughter Sayla love to sail in the Salish sea and create adventure stories together.

It's Okay to Be Perfectly Imperfect

Diane Jennings

"No, stop, don't do that, come here." I watched your eight-year-old little face screech at your six-year-old brother out of the back door. At that moment, I realised I was letting you down, I realised I was your role model and if I wanted you to grow up believing in yourselves, having confidence and resilience, I needed help.

I'd had a wonderful childhood, such a happy time with just me, my mum and my sister – a strong trio. I met your dad at the age of seventeen, sailed through exams, qualified as a children's nurse, got married, bought our first little house. Life was perfect, it was easy. We had it all, our whole life ahead of us.

Then bang! Motherhood. It was so hard. I hadn't expected it to be so hard. At the time I was a health visitor, I should have known what to do, I should have known how to be a good mum. But it was a struggle. You cried, you were sick, you cried some more. I felt helpless, I didn't know what had hit me.

We thought it would help if we had another baby. Your baby brother arrived much earlier than we had expected, he was so tiny and fragile. He was sick too, he spent weeks in hospital. All I could do was cry. Having two beautiful children was harder. The juggle and struggle was real. One day I was so frazzled I even drove out of the drive leaving one of you behind – who does that? I needed help.

I bumbled along, managing the best way I could, feeling lost, alone and tired; so tired. It took a brave colleague at work to make me realise I needed help. It took eight years of turmoil and stress for me to reach out. And I did and it was the best thing I ever did.

A supportive therapist helped me so much. It only took four sessions, and with the love of my beautiful family and a whole heap of time for me, I gained insight into my own emotional needs and realised that it was okay if things weren't perfect. I spent time with your dad, I found the wonderful benefits of self-care, had your baby brother, and I even trained to be a hypnotherapist.

It took me a long time to realise that it's okay to reach out for help, it's okay to say you're finding it difficult. Life is a journey, a rich tapestry. I've learnt so much along the way. Be kind, sprinkle it everywhere. Listen, listen to yourself, listen to others, listen to the silence. And, most of all, I want you to know there is no such thing as perfect; it's okay to be perfectly imperfect.

Diane Jennings lives in Lancashire with her amazing husband and three beautiful children. Her dream is to work full-time as a solution focused hypnotherapist. She thoroughly enjoys family time, yoga and running. Her aim is to run a marathon (or a half marathon at the least) before her joints decide she can't!

Self-Love Is Your Hidden Magic Wand

Nicoleta Rotaru

It was a late autumn day when I found out that I was going to have a baby angel. I didn't know what to do, the only thing I knew was that soon enough I would meet the love of my life.

And then I got to know that you were a girl, and that was the moment when I realised what a strong responsibility I had: to grow a strong woman out of you.

I didn't have the chance to be raised in an environment where I mattered, to receive words like 'good job!' 'You deserve this!' 'You're strong and beautiful, don't let anyone bring you down.'

No, none of these.

But, deep down, I knew that I was all of the above. I think my guardian angel whispered from time to time into my ears to not forget.

But with you, my dear Elina, I want something different. I want you to learn more about self-love and how much good it can bring to your life.

Forget about selfishness, that's not self-love, that's a lesson I'll teach you another time.

This is why I'm looking into your eyes so deeply when telling you 1000 times a day that you're beautiful, that your smile makes me happy.

I want you to understand your worth.

You don't need confirmation, that's for sure, but it's good to hear it, isn't it?

The power of words is incredible, and this is a lesson I've learned the hard way. Therefore, I want to ask you one little thing: to always remember my words, that you are beautiful in your unique way and do not let anyone tell you anything but this.

Do you know what else makes you special?

Your smile, my little soul. I love calling you the child of happiness because this is what you do, you put smiles on people's faces. You're kind and warm. You're pure joy and I can't get luckier than this.

And that's my lesson for you today: be aware of self-love.

Love yourself first to understand what love means. Don't be selfish, though. Let me help you grow into a beautiful and self-confident woman, let me guide you through this tough journey of life, let's be in this together.

Together we are stronger.

With love,

Mom

Nicoleta Rotaru is a twenty-seven-year-old mom who lives in a small town in Romania. She is a person who lives for creativity, explaining all her hobbies that made her bring in an extra income. Her passion for singing is beyond her own understanding and to this can also be added her passion for makeup, painting and, now, writing. She has just entered into the world of blogging thanks to her amazing boss who encouraged her that she is on the right track when building fashionable motherhood. Nicoleta is a full-time English teacher, but she thinks that life has different plans for her.

You Are Seen, You Are Heard, You Are Valued

Nikki Bruce

"Connection is the energy that exists between people when they feel seen, heard and valued; when they can give and receive without judgement."

Brené Brown

Noah,

Frank, your pet pug has just died and, as you sit and sob while I hold you in my arms, I wish I could take this pain away from you. You loved him and you miss him, and now he's gone you're trying to come to terms with it. This is the first time in your seven short years of navigating this world that you have had to confront something as devastating as death.

But that's the thing about life, there are all these big

feelings to feel, and I can't always protect you from them. I wish I could wrap you up and keep you safe from all the things that might hurt you and make you sad or angry, but I can't.

There is, however, one thing I can show you. The one thing that we all need and often lack – the power of connection. When we speak our thoughts and share our feelings, it helps us to make sense of them. This is especially true of the more insidious feelings that you might find creeping up on you as you grow into a young man. Societal pressures and different situations can make you feel hopeless and lost; when this happens, connecting with people you trust will help you find your way again.

The beauty of sharing these feelings is that other people will say 'me too!' and you'll see that you're not alone. These difficult feelings are all part of being human and sharing them will help you to see that we all feel them in some way, at some time.

Depression is a very real illness and one that unfortunately runs in our family. It can lie to you and make you feel sad, angry, or unworthy. You might sometimes feel like an outsider, disconnected from the people around you. When you feel like this the most important thing you can do, the thing that can help chase those feelings away, is to talk to somebody.

I hope you feel comfortable enough to share these feelings with me. I will help you take your power back from them and see them for what they are – lies and mistruths. It took me years to understand the power of sharing my feelings. Only recently, after making sense of my own feelings using therapy, have I discovered the power of challenging my thoughts and sharing my feelings with other people.

I will always be here to share your feelings with you. No matter how big, painful, or shameful they feel – together we will make sense of them.

Love Mommy

Hailing from Tamworth in the Midlands (UK) Nikki is a mom to Noah aged seven, a stepmom to Harmony aged five, and pet mom to Sully the pug. Nikki works in marketing and has always enjoyed writing creatively. She also loves festivals, gigs and cosy nights snuggled up on the sofa with her family.

Life Teaches You Lessons, Living Embraces Those Lessons

Clare Sirin

"Life can only be understood backwards but must be lived forwards."

Soren Keirkegaar

These words have resonated with me since the moment I came across them. As confusing as they may sound, I take great comfort knowing that learning backwards can sometimes be the only way to move forwards.

My story takes you on the journey I have travelled to get to today; discomfort and fear have been replaced with gratitude, comfort and a deep lying faith.

Growing up in Zimbabwe more than filled my cup.

Farm life was busy, there was always something new and exciting happening to fill a child's mind with intrigue and awe. Living according to the seasons, as all farmers do, we celebrated the rainfall and endured the drought. I had the privilege of space to explore, the freedom of safety, and a strong community whereby you were never alone. Home was my mecca through simple living in an abundant landscape.

Political unrest and turmoil turned our beloved country upside down and brought it to its knees. Our family was no longer welcome to stay. So, with my cat, our dog and my bicycle, Cape Town became home.

Here I met my husband; his positive, sunny personality brought the best out of me. He is a 'live in the moment' kind of guy. We drank in the beauty of the Cape, explored and adventured over and around the magnificent Table Mountain. Sea views and rugged cliffs, flowers of every description, and wind! "Wind is your friend," he would say, "face it head on, challenge it!"

And challenge it we did, in the form of a brain tumour.

It all happened so fast. He had the scan, the tumour was huge, he lay in ICU anticipating a twelve-hour brain surgery. What do you talk about? He comforted me, of course, the forever protector. "Don't worry, I guess it's time to do another Ironman, just follow the process!" And that is exactly what we did. One step at a time, we made it through two surgeries, a week in an induced coma, thirty days in hospital and a further three months of laying low. Only to be repeated a year later… that stubborn tumour grew back!

Fast forward fourteen years and it's all about living in the moment, appreciating the hard times and wow, celebrating and loving the great times. We have been married for thirteen years, have two beautiful children, the roller coaster ride continues with further surgeries, radiation, seizures and everything that goes with it. We are certainly living forwards and learning backwards, but we've got it! The many mountains we have climbed have become our assets and the wind has become my friend!

To my precious children, life may not take the route you expect, and it will more than likely be patterned with lumps and bumps. Living and learning, understanding and embracing will sometimes feel back to front like it did for Dad and me! Ask those underlying questions but try starting them with a 'what' and not a 'why'. Be open to change and find joy and comfort in the 'simples', because on the scary days, the simples will be your biggest comforts.

Clare Sirin lives in Cape Town, South Africa. She is wife to Avron and mum to Benjamin and Rebecca. Growing up on a farm in Zimbabwe, she realised her love for flowers would be a life-long love affair. From admiring their effortless beauty to appreciating their consistent perseverance to thrive, she has created a business, Msasa Design, to reflect these unique learnings.

You Are Your Number One

Jemma Andrew-Adiamah

Three weeks into being a mum of two and the days felt long with an unrelenting mix of breastfeeding, being tied to a breast pump, nappies, toddler life and the usual day-to-day grind.

I was in autopilot mode to survive those sleep-deprived days to make it through.

Amongst all of that, I was also running my business as a full-time blogger and studying for my coaching certification.

Let's be REAL, it wasn't easy, and looking back I'm not sure how it was possible.

It was tough, exhausting and the days felt long. At times I became resentful of the situation that I couldn't do more. Nothing I did felt good enough because there wasn't any available time to really dedicate to my passions. I felt stagnant and like I was losing a piece of myself each day.

Studying for my coaching certification was tough, but

I was determined to keep the work up, not only because I wanted to serve and support mums on a deeper level, but I wanted a sliver of something for myself too.

In those moments that I had in between bedtime and the baby's next feed, I felt:

- Empowered because I was doing something that I knew would help other mums like me.
- Purposeful and fulfilled because I'd carved out time just for me.
- Joyous because I was doing something I loved.
- Like ME, for the simple fact that it was something for myself, outside of being a mum.

It's so easy to lose the essence of who you are when you become a mum, but for me, it was non-negotiable.

I knew if I was to truly thrive in motherhood, I needed to stay connected and true to myself because I MATTER TOO…

… as do YOU.

I've come to the conclusion that I'm actually a better parent when I'm living my life on my terms and prioritising myself. When I feel my best by honouring my needs, it means everyone and everything gets the best – my husband, kids, house, plants… everything.

Just because you've become a mum, it doesn't mean that you start taking care of yourself any less. You actually need to be dialing up that self-care because there's not just you to look after now, there are these little humans relying on you and a family.

There should be no guilt for this self-LESS act.

This is the lesson that I want to pass on to my own children because they're a reflection of my learned behaviours and beliefs. If their norm is to see me constantly forgetting about myself and putting myself at the bottom of the to-do list, eventually that will become their reality too.

I don't want that for me or for them.

Through observational learning, children can pick up on the most subtle of behaviours sometimes modelled unknowingly by their parents.

It's time to break the cycle.

Jemma Andrew-Adiamah is a mum of two and lives in Nottinghamshire. She's a holistic Empowerment Coach that helps unfulfilled mums to put themselves first without the guilt. She helps mums feel fabulous, achieve the mental clarity they need to reconnect with themselves and rediscover their ambitions so that they can step into a fulfilling and joyful life while balancing mamahood.

Listen to Your Heart – It Knows the Way!

Tracey Hutchinson

I always knew the type of parent I would be – children needed structure, guidance and boundaries. I loved Super Nanny and her techniques. Until I had my first child – and realised that I really didn't want to parent from a place of control and fear. I read parenting books aplenty and it was these books that introduced me to a peaceful way to parent.

My eldest daughter was super strong-willed. I loved and embraced it. I was determined to allow her to be her authentic self and to follow her own heart. It wasn't always easy. Hell, it was never easy! I learnt so many amazing lessons from this little one – and still am ten years later! I learnt to surrender, to let it go, to trust that she knew what was best for her, to make my own decisions from a place of love, not fear. She didn't come into the world a blank slate.

She has so much wisdom and knowing within her and my role is to allow her to stay connected to this.

Early on in my parenting journey, I was led to books that taught me the importance of allowing all emotions and accepting them without judgement, thus allowing them to be felt fully and to dissipate. As a result of this, my daughter was more emotionally mature than most adults I'd ever known. When I finally began to love myself as the perfectly imperfect parent that I was, I allowed myself the same courtesy of holding space for all my emotions without judgement and this was a total game changer for me. To be okay with where I was, even if my actions did not meet my 'ideal' standard. To appreciate all the ways in which I was the most beautiful parent ever, rocking parenting the best I could with the information that I had available at each stage. As we all do!

When Coronavirus struck in 2020, my family experienced one of my most favourite manifestations of listening to our hearts. Seven months pregnant, I was thrilled when schools closed down and we got to have my eldest daughter at home 24/7. School work was overwhelming, and we quickly dropped it in place of us doing our own thing. This was our opportunity to see what home education would be like – something I'd been curious about for a while.

We all adored the freedom (which ironically most of the world wasn't enjoying at this difficult time), and loved directing our own day, following our impulses and spending so much quality time together as a family. I was thrilled when my daughter announced her plans to be home educated permanently. We are all enjoying this new journey –and each one of us is learning plenty along the way.

The birth of my second daughter reminded me that we are never the finished product. There will be more lessons, more surrendering, more opportunities to draw on the trust I have in the flow of life. Connecting to my inner guidance and listening to my heart has led to so much ease and joy in my family. My parenting journey has unfolded perfectly, and I love encouraging my daughters to listen to their own hearts. They won't always have me to guide them, but they will always have their own inner guidance. And no one knows us better than we know ourselves.

Tracey Hutchinson lives in Leicestershire, UK, and is a wife and an unschooling mum to two incredible girls – ten and one. She loves nothing more than to support mums to go beyond traditional parenting, into the realms of parenting in the present moment with Joy, Ease, Love and Connection. As a Clarity Coach, she uses Gina Mallison's Evoke Method, which enables clients to release negative feelings, thoughts and beliefs around a particular topic and come into alignment with their own inner guidance system.

It Is Okay to Not Be Okay

Sarah Wilson

I am a firm believer that you should look for the positives in life. Every cloud has a silver lining. When it rains, look for rainbows. However, life isn't all sunshine and rainbows. Sometimes there are storm clouds; big black swirling ones that make it seem near impossible to see the light. In these moments, I want you to know it is okay to not be okay.

In society today there is so much pressure to be happy. A sea of smiling faces with their picture-perfect lives on social media. A world where influencers try to sell an aspirational lifestyle #livingmybestlife. Even the standard British greeting of "how are you?" expects a positive response, that at the very least you are "fine, thanks".

I spent too many years pretending I was fine. A chronic illness diagnosis aged eleven started a desperate battle to be "normal". Rather than confronting my new reality and the complex set of thoughts and emotions it triggered, I painted a smile on my face. I congratulated myself on convincing the outside world that I was just like them, that I was doing just fine. I mistakenly thought this charade was a show of strength. I was wrong. I have learned that true strength lies in acknowledging and sharing how you are feeling. Sometimes the bravest thing you can do is to say "I am not okay".

Being vulnerable is hard. I found taking off the carefully crafted mask I wore and letting people see all the parts I had kept hidden a challenging process. My hope for you is that you never feel the need to put on the mask in the first place. You are entitled to your feelings, all of them. You should never suffer in silence. It doesn't matter if the problem doesn't have a solution, or if it feels small compared to other people's issues or you have no idea why you feel the way you do. You are loved and valued for all that you are, and being happy is not a prerequisite. Everyone experiences moments of sadness, anger and frustration; these moments do not define you.

Sometimes when the storm front rolls in and it starts to pour, you can embrace it; dance in the rain, splash in puddles and look for rainbows. Other times it is just dark and cold and wet, and no amount of positivity will change this. Embrace this too, safe in the knowledge sometimes it is okay to not be okay.

Sarah Wilson is a mum to two incredible sons, who are her world. She calls the vibrant city of Bristol (UK) home with her husband, their boys and rescue cat. She is a country girl at heart having grown up in rural Norfolk, so can often be found pottering in the garden, covered in mud! After many years working in the financial sector, motherhood has given her the courage to find the escape hatch and embark on a new adventure with the goal of helping people.

You Can Do Anything You Set Your Mind To

Tiphany Janik

My fifth-grade teacher was pretty humdrum for the most part, but he did get excited when it came to his science projects. He would award a few of the excelling students with a fun science experiment held in the back of the class, while the majority of the students were assigned busy work. As a hands-on learner, this was agonizing.

I recall a vivid memory of sitting at my desk in the front of the classroom on one of those Friday so-called 'fun days' and looking at a couple of corny motivational posters on the wall.

'Believe and Achieve.'

'You Can Do Anything You Set Your Mind To.'

I admit, I thought the messages were nice, but I also knew deep down they weren't meant for me. They were there for the 'smart' kids in the class; the high achievers.

I had low self-esteem for what seemed to be the majority of my life. Instead of empowering messages, I carried around limiting beliefs such as:

'If it doesn't come easy, I'll never be good at it.'

'To fail means I AM a failure.'

'I am dumb.'

By having a fixed mindset, I resisted taking on anything that sounded too risky for the fear of looking dumb. I especially didn't want to let anyone I fooled into thinking I was smart to know the real truth. I carried this limiting mindset well into my adult years.

Just a couple of years ago, I made a difficult choice to stop home schooling my five children and start a business. This situation forced me to challenge many of my limiting beliefs. Starting a business meant trying new things. Trying new things meant making mistakes. Making mistakes meant, well… looking dumb.

It was in this decision of making this major life change that I felt I had no choice but to get uncomfortable and try new things. To my surprise, I began to not fear mistakes but to use each one as an opportunity to learn from them. I began to take on a growth mindset.

In this seemingly short amount of time, I have grown closer to becoming the person I've only dreamed to be. I've also discovered work that I find fulfilling and meaningful. Though nothing can ever replace my first and foremost passion of being a mother.

Funnily enough now, I have taken on the role of

spreading messages similar to the ones found on those corny motivational posters that I used to find outlandish.

I want my kids to not be afraid to make mistakes but to take every mistake as an opportunity to learn from them and grow stronger and wiser. I want them to persevere even when the going gets tough. And when they read powerful statements on motivational posters, like I read that day, I want them to know deep down that it truly IS meant for them!

Tiphany Janik lives in sunny California raising five amazing kids alongside her ever-supporting husband from Poland. She is a life coach and the founder of Best Self Mom, a self-improvement and wellness blog where she shares tools and strategies on topics like self-care, mindset, goals, habits and more!

You Are Beautiful, Both Inside and Out

Vicki Lowes

"Baby, baby pigtails!"

A response from a girl in the year above me to my hairstyle of choice at the age of just seven.

"I didn't know you were pregnant!"

A comment made by one of my peers in Year 6 when I wore a pencil skirt to school instead of my usual leggings. I was underweight at the time, but always had a protruding stomach and had since birth.

"You look like a witch with your pointy nose, chin and grey hair!"

A remark made by a so-called friend at random while we were in the playground in the first year of secondary school. My hair wasn't grey; it was a sort of dull, mousy-brown shade.

"She's Primark; I'm Gucci."

A bitter declaration by someone, confused by someone else's attraction to me.

From a young age, I realised that a proportion of people would judge me (and others) based on appearance first and foremost. At a similar time, I also discovered that I had a penchant for supporting people and unfortunately, due to my caring nature, I would often get taken for granted or used.

With the media obsessing over people's looks and weight gain or loss, it is no wonder why us women can focus on that over our personality, our behaviour, our complete selves. I distinctly remember the 'Fatt Le Blanc' headlines when the '90s heartthrob, Joey from *Friends*, gained a little weight. The 'Blobby Williams' one stands out, too. The more times you see people, whatever their gender, their age, their ethnicity, their career, being judged against superficial criteria, the greater the message that appearance is the ultimate indicator of success is compounded into your brain.

Doughnuts are a huge hit with my daughters. I could buy the tastiest looking ones, you know the ones with shimmering pink icing and lashings of hundreds and thousands (the ones that I would love to shove my face straight into in the supermarket car park). But imagine if the inside contained something unappealing; the girls would refuse to eat them. Who can blame them? Yes, I'm making a comparison between a human and a doughnut. It is true, though. You could be the most stunningly beautiful person to look at, but if you have a vacuous personality and treat people unfairly, people will soon realise your true value.

When it comes to true value, from a young age, I have always tried to be kind and do my best to help others. Goodness, it sounds like I'm quoting the Brownie Guide Law right there, and perhaps that is where my service to others began. Far from perfect, I've made mistakes along the way, but I maintain that being someone who strives to support others, rather than knocking them down, and giving to others, not expecting anything back, is far more important than having blemish-free skin and a perfectly toned physique.

My daughters are currently aged eight and five. At the moment, they have no inhibitions about the way they look. However, inevitably, as they get older, they will develop insecurities; these are natural. Both now and when that moment comes, my message to them is:

"You ARE always enough. You are beautiful, both inside and out. Be true to yourselves. I am proud of you both."

Vicki Lowes is mum to two fantastic daughters, rainbow babies who changed her life. She lives in Norfolk, but maintains a firm 'proud to be northern' attitude, calling North Yorkshire home, despite not having been resident there for over half of her life. Vicki is a qualified primary school teacher, currently working part-time with older students in a complex needs setting. She also has her own education and tuition business, Blossom Education.

Don't Let Anything Hold You Back

Sally Sarson

I see you, standing there on the sidelines, wanting to join in but fear and self-doubt is holding you back.

I see you, I feel you, I am you.

The one thing no one tells you when you become a mum is that you give birth to a piece of your heart, it's handed to you right there in the delivery room wrapped up in a soft blanket. My world changed forever the day I became your mum, and I had no idea what I was doing.

Yeah, sure, I'd read lots of baby books, I'd looked after my niece and nephews when they were young babies, but nothing prepares you for that moment when you give birth to your very own tiny human.

The early years were good, you hit all the milestones with ease, and it wasn't until you first started school that

I realised I'd given you something from me, from my childhood, and that something was fear and self-doubt.

As a child I was massively lacking in self-confidence, I was the incredibly shy girl, the one that feared putting her hand up in class in case she got the answer wrong and everyone laughed. The girl with the bright auburn curly hair, the freckles, the wonky nose and the national health glasses that she hated with a passion.

This fear and shyness carried with me all through my school years. Yeah, sure, I was confident around my close friends, but I got anxious about meeting new people and I never mixed that well with others. There were often times when I really wanted to do things, wanted to join in but I let my fear hold me back and I never got to enjoy some things as a child I probably should have.

They say the school years are the best years of your life and looking back I did enjoy school, I just wished I'd known back then as I do now that by letting go of my fear I could have enjoyed so much more and explored new opportunities.

All any mum wants is the best for their child, they want to see you grow and enjoy a carefree life.

So, I say this to you now with love, let go of that fear every now and then, push yourself to try new things. Yes, it'll be hard at first, but I'm here for you.

I'll always be here for you and, if you ever fall, I'll be there to catch you.

Sally lives in Leicestershire in the UK with her husband and two daughters. An avid reader, Sally can often be found with her head in a book and usually has two or three books on the go at any one time. Sally runs her own Etsy shop called Sallybee Designs where she sells bespoke personalised gifts for all occasions.

Create Intentions, Visions and Possibilities

Jane Tyson

As I walked alone through gate three at Heathrow aged twenty, tearfully waving goodbye to my mum, dad, sister and grandad, I was simultaneously filled with delight that I'd actually done it, it was happening, I was heading to Oz!

Grandad Mike had always shared stories about his two-year adventure as a '£10 pom' heading off on the big cruise liner to Australia in the 1960s. He too went solo, quickly making lifelong friends with the Millar family who he met during breakfast, later becoming godfather to the youngest, Michael.

He took on jobs of window cleaning, gold mining (he claimed the sweat from this hard work gave him the hairs on his chest) and ploughing fields throughout the night, whilst living in a small shed full of spiders! His stories of overcoming challenges inspired Auntie Kay and me.

Communication was difficult, he was reliant only on the postal service to hear news of his loved one, i.e. Nanny Carol back in the UK, and many times he felt lonely and homesick.

In 1992, during my backpacking adventure, I hadn't heard of email. Instead I'd regularly head to the next post office "restaurante" in whatever town I was working in or backpackers I was staying at to excitedly read my handwritten mail from friends and family. This connection meant a lot.

I'd set a goal when I was thirteen to have this adventure and had saved up with the various random jobs I had. I wrote it down with a timeline, alongside other wishes, including buying a sofa, ha! I was inspired by Grandad and also the book he'd dip into and share with us *Think and Grow Rich* by Napoleon Hill, which I too keep next to my bed. It has served me in pursuing a "richness" of life minus the millions. "One day, Rodney!" as Grandad would say!

Nanny Carol also travelled to America for a short while and this is something I would encourage you to interview her about. Collect stories from your relatives, as they teach us about life lessons and how they dusted themselves off when things got tough.

I even wrote down a goal to have you two and visualised you both in my mind. By the way, your names mean "light". One day when you are ready, I'll share your life codes.

It's good to create intentions, vision and possibilities. Life will have many curveballs; look up, breathe and glance wide.

I still write in my affirmation and goal-setting book. For example, in 2014 I wrote "we live in a quirky house, with a beautiful view and my children play out freely". It also included that I climb Mount Kilimanjaro. I wrote this freely without logic, just feeling and believing.

Six months later, as you know, I had a teaching job at an International School in Tanzania and your dad took an extended sabbatical from the news desk. We found ourselves living in a house on campus, opposite a volcano and you were running around freely with new friends. It was a magical family adventure that touched us all in so many ways, would you agree?

So, take some time to explore what you would like to BE, Say, Do and Have too, then write them down, with a date, and see what happens.

Mum x

Jane Tyson lives in Guildford with her husband, a journalist, and two teenagers. Teacher and founder of Resilient Kids. Boosting VISION, VITALITY AND VOICE.

Don't Walk Our Path, Pave a New Better Road

Sarah Horgan

I sit here and try to explain my reasons and reassure you that I am not doing it to be mean, or be that evil stepmum, but more so because I actually care and want the best for you and your health. You do not want to have to go through the health struggles that your father has. I would not wish that upon anyone. And if there is one thing I can do for you to give you the best chance at avoiding having to go through these health struggles, it is to teach you the importance of eating well, loving healthy food and to set the foundation for your overall health now and into your adult life.

While you may not quite understand now, one day you will thank me. Trust me!

As he starts to calm down, I can still see the slight frustration, yet I can see my stepson really listening to me.

You have seen the struggles that your father has gone through, the lack of energy he has some days, how he has to run to the toilet after eating certain foods, the recent hospital visits and nearly losing his bowel. Luckily, we are learning to manage this now.

Crohn's disease tends to run in families, making your chance of developing it much higher. That's not to scare you at all, but rather just make you aware. This is why I am always so on to you about telling me of any bowel changes you may have and the food you may have eaten.

When we were kids, our parents didn't have the knowledge that is available to us today, growing up on a diet full of processed packaged foods and sugar, yet very little emphasis on veggies. I mean we were told to eat our veggies, but I don't think they really knew the true significance it would have on our health and dietary patterns into adulthood.

I myself have gone through my fair share of gut issues and I look back now and can really see the connections that my food and lifestyle choices have had on this.

While we still don't know the true cause of Crohn's, we do believe that diet, along with many lifestyle factors, have been contributors to the development and severity of this disease.

It is my gift to you, as your stepmum, to do everything I can, to give you the best start in life while you are still young, to provide you with the knowledge that I have that is going to help you adopt healthy food choices for life, while still knowing a treat every now and then is not going to do harm. I am also here to teach you to listen to your body. When a food doesn't make you feel good, know that this may be your body trying to tell you to listen to it. As a parent I will do everything in my power to set you up for good health, while doing the best I can to reduce your risk factor of developing Crohn's Disease, an illness that affects both your parents, that at times can be quite debilitating.

Everything I do for you, I do as if you were my very own. My wish for you is that you always have health and happiness.

Sarah Horgan is a stepmum to an energetic ten-year-old boy from Adelaide South Australia. As a Nutritionist, she believes strongly in food as medicine. When she took on the role of mum, she knew that all she wanted to do was bring him up the exact same way she would as if he was her own. Adopting healthy eating habits in our kids is essential for their health, not only in their early years, but all the way up into adulthood. Sarah is a Gut Health Nutritionist for mums and founder of Nutritious Vitality.

When You Believe in Yourself, Anything Is Possible

Nicky Masson

It took me until I was in my mid-thirties to believe in myself.

Throughout my life I had developed a coping mechanism, which was to tell myself that I was strong, and that even though I had been through some pretty unspeakable things, it was okay and that these things had happened. It was kind of that British stiff upper lip mentality of 'let's just soldier on' and 'I'm fine'.

I didn't want to acknowledge my past in the hope it would disappear. What I really wanted to do was to try and forget it, but I didn't realise that I was suppressing those feelings and they would lie dormant. But, of course, just like a volcano, it has to erupt at some point.

It wasn't until I had my children that all of my unresolved

emotional baggage came flooding to the surface. I had post-natal depression, which hit me like a tonne of bricks, bad anxiety and I was frustrated, sad and angry.

I didn't feel like me at all – almost like a shadow of myself. Inside I wanted to scream for help, but I would never have been able to get the words out. I just couldn't make sense of it all and I constantly felt like a failure and a bad mum. At that point I felt like my life might be like that forever.

For so many years I had pretended to be strong but what I was really doing was masking the pain. However, all of that did change when I made the decision that enough was enough and a chance meeting with a coach changed the direction of my life forever. From them on I knew that I needed to find a way forward. I had to deal with the past and in doing so not only did I heal myself, but I also learnt how to help others do the same. I was fascinated by how the mind works, became a coach and specialised in Emotional Intelligence.

This was a huge turning point for me. My self-worth and self-esteem went up, my confidence grew, and I started to believe in myself for the first time ever and it showed in all areas of my life.

My relationships improved, I grew a successful business, and I was happy and making plans for the future.

Now my purpose in life is to show others that they don't need to be defined by their past, and that they can be, do or have anything they want.

I grew up with a lifetime of trauma because I didn't

know another way, but my hope is that my boys have a better understanding of their emotions and how to manage them, and above all else that they believe in themselves.

Because when you believe in yourself, anything is possible.

Nicky Masson lives in Market Harborough with her husband and two boys, Hugo and Harrison. She is a Business Coach helping female entrepreneurs to grow a thriving business without compromising on family time. She is also a big advocate for mental health awareness, loves to support small businesses, and likes a good cup of coffee!

Be Anything but Nice

Jessica Haberman

When I was growing up, I was the nice girl. Oh, that's Jessica, she's so nice. It was a compliment for the most part, and I was happy to live up to that expectation. Coming from a small, rural area, this was easy enough. There weren't a lot of differing opinions about what nice meant and the circle of influence wasn't very large. Family, friends, teachers, coaches were all mostly the same people in various roles. I was also fairly shy and "being nice" was a safe place to hide, where I didn't have to share my opinions or let myself be fully known.

Moving on to college and out into the large world, being "nice" became problematic. As it turns out, it's a very subjective word. When in a larger pool of influence with more diverse experiences and backgrounds, nice means different things to different people. I had not broken it down into what it meant for me, and it led to a bit of an identity crisis. I had to figure out who I was without being able to use "nice" as a crutch. It was confusing but ultimately led to the path of figuring out myself and who I am rather than focusing so much on making everyone around me happy. I learned, sadly not very quickly, that when I am trying to please everyone, I'm not pleasing anyone at all. Especially not myself.

Words have meanings attached to them and I believe the meanings hold power, making it important to be purposeful about the way we think about ourselves. The more I think about the word "nice", the more problems I find with it. People often use the word nice when they can't come up with anything better to say, giving the impression of blandness, mediocrity, forgettable. Boring. It is also a word that can be charged with sarcasm. "Nice" is frequently used after making a mistake or when something negative happens. Even if used as a compliment, I think there is an endless number of words to choose to describe our lovely selves that are more dynamic, clear and tangible.

As for my children, while I hope their father and I are raising them to be kind, compassionate and brave, I don't want them to entertain the thought of being "nice". Growing up and leaving home probably always leads to a bit of an identity crisis, but I want my kids to have more of a foundational knowledge of who they are at heart. I think that can be encouraged by naming their gifts and strengths with clear language and celebrating what makes them unique. I'm hoping to give them the vocabulary to be able to describe themselves when the world feels big and overwhelming. Joyful? Yes. Strong willed? Yes. Curious? Yes. Nice? No thank you.

Jessica Haberman lives on a small farm in Washington State with her family. She is the mom of four littles aged four and under. Her husband is an entrepreneur, which has led to many adventures together. She works as an emergency nurse and enjoys writing on the blog for Storyteller Farm.

Never Give Up. Your Differences Don't Mean You Can't Be the Best Person You Can Be

Suzi Shaw

I hope that this shares some memories, stories and messages I want my children to remember and live by. Never give up. No matter what is thrown at you or how hard you find something, keep going. It may not be the same journey as someone else, it may have to be done differently or adapted, but you can still do it and still be the best person you can be, even working with the difficulties you may face.

Motherhood has been done differently by me in

comparison to other mums. For example, I have never been able to run around and climb trees with them (due to mobility issues and illness), never been able to afford for them to go to dance or swimming classes (we didn't have the money), we didn't live anywhere we loved until about six years ago (due to being emergency housed as we were homeless – we were just so grateful for a roof over our babies' heads). Things have been tough, not only for my husband and me, but also for the three most amazing people who I couldn't be prouder of, my babies (now twenty, seventeen and sixteen).

My husband has been dealing with mental illness for most of the twenty-two years we've been together. He's had a couple of breakdowns and been in a state where he was unable to get out of bed for months. At that point, I had three children – three, fifteen months and a baby – postnatal depression for the third time (no one tells you it can hit you in different ways), whilst trying to hold everything together and be the 'perfect mother'. With help from my health visitor and 'Home-Start' (a brilliant charity supporting families when things are tough), I learnt that a 'perfect mother' doesn't exist, I needed to stop comparing myself to this image and I needed to do what was right for my family. We spent time doing silly things like playing on swings, going down slides, walking by the river, collecting conkers and making daisy chains.

My babies and I did things differently, preferring to play with language (love notes sometimes English, sometimes Latin, inside their lunchboxes), putting on puppet shows and telling stories. We talked about my 'invisible dragon' who watched out for them when we weren't together, sang songs on walks, went dinosaur hunting in the woods, had "good girl raisins" to help our youngest (and laziest) to walk, rather than be carried.

Despite having seen various health issues (their own, my husband's and mine), they've never let it faze them. My physical health has deteriorated from walking unaided to using a rollator (affectionately called 'Wally') to now using crutches. They've always picked up the things I drop or got pans out of cupboards.

'Disability' means you might have to do things differently. It also means we're more open to talking about disability, pain, degeneration and mental health. They know not to judge from the outside, to give everyone a chance.

Always remember to never give up. Things might happen that make your tasks or journey seem impossible, but there's always another way. Make adaptations and still be the best person you can be and achieve anything you want to. You are amazing. I believe in you.

Suzi Shaw, an ex-teacher living in Surrey, runs a forum for those with mental illnesses ('Dealing With Depression'). She has multiple chronic conditions including fibromyalgia, osteoarthritis and ADHD. Her children are aged 20, 17 and 16 and they have disabilities including ASD, dyslexia and EDS. She lives with her husband, children and dogs.

Your Voice Is Your Power

Liz Johnson

As a child, I saw the world as a multisensory kaleidoscope, and I was fascinated by it all. I absorbed all that color, light and sound, added my own pizazz, and by age three I was ready to take this show on the road. I escaped frequently from the comforts of home to seek adventure, approaching strangers on the street to share my favorite songs and stories. I might have become the next Shirley Temple – even had the dimples – but, unfortunately, no Hollywood producer ever knocked at my door.

I became a star at school where I dazzled the teachers, although my classmates were my harshest critics. I was a nobody on the playground. Those were the good days. On bad days, I was a target.

At home, I was one of five, a middle child, easily overlooked if I kept my head down and followed the rules, but instead I pushed boundaries, always devising some scheme, experiment or prank. I was swirling with creative energy demanding an outlet but there were few options. Ours was a quiet house. My dad suffered from PTSD, a souvenir of World War Two, and so my mom's primary job was to keep the children quiet. My exuberance was suppressed, and my voice was silenced.

I took refuge in my room, escaping into books and music, but my questions went unasked, ideas unspoken, feelings repressed. I retreated into my inner world, plagued with self-doubt, which escalated into chronic anxiety.

Later, school allowed me to explore other avenues of expression through art, theater, music, photography and filmmaking, but all my unresolved emotional baggage was bursting at the seams. Anxiety completely ruled my life until even leaving my room became too big a risk.

"Fear is the illness. Love is the cure."

Bobby Mattingly

I met and married a man whose love and support helped me to stay grounded. He made me laugh when I took things too seriously. When I became a mom, I knew I had to unlearn my old patterns to be emotionally available for my children. I found inspiration in books and found healing in nature. I learned how to let go, shaking off all the cobwebs of fear and doubt that caused my anxiety. I could be free to share my creative energy with my children through songs, stories and adventures. I had found my voice again.

I went on to work in classrooms, camps and after-school programs teaching art, writing and drama, where

I encouraged hundreds of children to use their voices. In the community, I painted murals, organized events and supported others in speaking their truth. I've even read my poetry aloud on occasion. By using my voice, I reclaimed my power and helped others to find their own.

My children have grown to be caring and creative adults who have often doubted themselves and their place in the world, but I hope they know how much our world needs their unique perspective, their heart, their passion, that spark that can illuminate a new path for the future. Our voice is our power.

one voice can break the silence
one light can quell the darkness
one word can inspire a generation
one life can change the world

Liz Johnson is a lifelong learner and educator with interests in writing, art, photography and the natural world. She actively supports local and global efforts to build community and is an advocate for the well-being of children and the environment. She has raised two children and lives with her husband in Philadelphia, PA.

Everything Happens for a Reason

Jen Parker

It took me a long time to realise that I am a bit of a control freak. While this has its benefits, like helping me run my own business well, it also has its downsides. I'm not a great passenger in a car, I struggle to relax when someone else is doing my make up and I wasn't great at delegating when I was a manager. The hardest thing, though, is when events or situations occur that are beyond my control.

One of those events was getting diagnosed with inflammatory arthritis in my early twenties. It halted my dream career of going into the police before it even started. Dealing with the challenges of finding the right medications and the balance of keeping active whilst not overdoing it has certainly put my positive mental attitude to the test over the years! The biggest challenge to date, though, was losing my mum in March 2019. Lily, you were only two, but having seen Nanny pretty much every day since you were born meant you had an incredible bond. Amber, you were only three months old, but I will forever be grateful that you got to meet Nanny and she got to hold you and celebrate your birth with us.

All of these challenges were beyond my control, and at times, I really struggled to deal with them. When Nanny died, I was utterly heartbroken, and I had no idea how I was going to make it through and be the best mum I could be to you two beautiful girls without her. The truth was that I needed help. Daddy was a huge support to me, as always, but I needed more help. I had to be honest with the GP that I was struggling to cope, and I was prescribed antidepressants to reduce my anxiety. I also had great support from family and friends. But probably the best thing I did was to say yes to grief counselling.

It allowed me to see that while it is great to have a positive attitude, you also have to accept negative feelings in order to process them too. I had to deal with the fact that Nanny's illness was out of my control, but how I reacted wasn't. I needed to grieve, I needed to cry, I needed to feel angry. Once I realised that it was okay to feel those negative emotions, it was easier to deal with them and allow myself to feel happy again.

Nanny always said, 'everything happens for a reason', but that is difficult to see when such awful things can happen. However, I am coming round to the idea more and more. Without my arthritis I may never have started my own business, as needing more control over my health was the push I needed. It also meant I needed c-sections to give birth to you both, and Lily, you had hidden complications in my tummy that meant if I'd gone for a natural birth, you may not have made it, which Nanny said was the biggest reason of all for me having this disease! Losing her was the hardest thing I've ever been through, but it's also made me realise I'm stronger than I thought, and she will always inspire me to be the best mum I can be.

Jen Parker lives in Leicestershire with her husband and kids, two girls, aged four and two, and her beloved pooch Doug the shug (a pug shih-tzu cross). Having worked in the book publishing industry for over eleven years, Jen made the move to start her own business in September 2017 at the end of her first maternity leave and now supports authors looking to self-publish beautiful books with her editing, design and publishing services. She had the honour of producing this book as well as contributing to it!

Appendix

Write Your Own Story to Share with Your Child – and The World

You've read the book, now it's your turn to write your story. Follow the short guide below to write your piece and then send it to us so that we can share it on our social media and blog. And you never know, you could even be part of our next book!

Just follow these steps:

1. Ask yourself: What is the one life meaning I would love my child to learn from me? It could be a belief, value, purpose or passion that's important to you or has marked your life in some way.
2. Reflect on the moment(s) and anecdotes in your life that lead you to that life meaning.
3. Write a piece of up to 600 words that portrays your life meaning, relating those moments from your life

that have given the foundations of your belief, value, purpose or passion.

4. Give it a title that reflects your life meaning. It needs to read like the message you want to tell your child.
5. Write a short bio (around 50 words) in the third person giving some details of who you are, where you're from, your hobbies, work, etc. But, if you prefer, you can remain totally anonymous.
6. Include a photo for us to use alongside your story on our social media and blog. This is totally optional; we can publish your story without any photo.

Then send it all over to us via:

www.meaningsovermilestones.me

I can't wait to read your story!

Angharad

Acknowledgements

This book would be just a pretty cover if it weren't for each and every one of the co-authors who not only wrote their stories for the book, but helped crowd-fund for its production and were integral to spreading the word on its very existence. Thank you authors for sharing with us your stories, your hearts.

Thanks to pure fate for helping me find my amazing editor, Jen Parker of Fuzzy Flamingo. This book was just an idea at the back of my mind and one that I felt sure I didn't have the knowledge or resources to undertake. Thank you, Jen, your work and support have made my scribble of an idea in a notebook a reality.

Thanks to my wonderfully supportive husband, who is my biggest cheerleader. His unwavering belief in me and my dreams are what fuels me on the days when I feel like the mountain is just too big a climb. Thanks to listening to my endless rants and worries. And to helping me realise my life-long dreams.

My beautiful sons, you are the reason I do what I do every day. You are who I want to change the world for. You are my absolute everything. Thank you for being who you are and for making me a mum.

The roots and wings, which have made me me, I owe to my parents. Thank you for letting me forge my own path without judgement and with total support, even when secretly you probably wished I wasn't doing half of what I was! I can't thank you enough for giving me that freedom to explore, to learn, to be me and to always be there when I fall. Thank you.

Thanks to the little boy who changed my world when I was twenty years old. Your strength, grace and humility is something I try to emulate each and every day. You planted the seed of my life purpose and the beliefs I hold most dear.

And thanks to all the people, too many to mention here, who are in my life today and who have played even the smallest part along the years. Thank you to the very many strangers who have made me smile at a moment I needed it or have helped me out when I was struggling. I truly believe that each encounter with every single person has brought me to this very moment today.

So, to you all, a big thank you.

Printed in Great Britain
by Amazon

65109122R00132